HOLIDAYS AND PRAYERS
חַגִּים וּתְפִלּוֹת

by

Sol Scharfstein

KTAV Publishing House, Inc.,

This book is lovingly dedicated to
my
grandchildren
Alyssa
Danielle
David
Jeffrey
Lauren
Matthew
Zachary

Printed in China
KTAV Publishing House, Inc.
930 Newark Street
Jersey City, NJ 07306
Copyright® 2005
ISBN 0-88125-883-0

TABLE OF CONTENTS

Introduction

Shalom Haverim

To know the Jewish way of life, you must know your history, how your faith came to be, its language, and how to memorialize it with celebration and prayer.

Holidays and Prayers will take you on an exciting flight through history and a panoramic journey through a rainbow of holidays. On your 4,000-year journey, you will meet heroes and heroines who fought for the freedom to worship and for the right to exist as a sovereign nation. You will visit with prophets and scribes who gave us a code of religious laws that which governs our religious, social, and philanthropic institutions.

The road our people have traveled in both distance and spirit is long and varied. You are a part of a people that has existed for 4,000 years in numerous, mostly inhospitable, regions. You carry the genes of Moses the lawgiver, David the warrior, the strength and resolve of the matriarchs and the patriachs. You carry the DNA of the prophets, the rabbis, the heroes of the Warsaw ghetto, the Russian refusniks who resisted communism, and the Israelis who defeated the armies of ten Arab nations that tried to destroy our dreams of liberty and sovereignty. Now it's your turn to step up and learn about your noble heritage, and as knowledgeable Jews, become the future leaders of our people.

ABOUT THE TEXT

Your book, Holidays and Prayers is a multifaceted text specifically designed to coordinate and teach Jewish history, Jewish customs and ceremonies, and Jewish home and synagogue prayers as a single learning experience.

Holidays and Prayers consists of sixteen major units. Most of the units are divided into six secondary sections.

1. Why Holidays?

These essays review the history of holidays. The texts are integrated with a basic Hebrew vocabulary from the Word Bank.

2. Let's Celebrate_____.

Reviews the sources and customs and how to celebrate the holiday

3. Home Prayers

Basic candle-lighting and Kiddush prayers. All the prayers are preceded by an introductory paragraph, that explains the context. Your prayer book contains prayers for different occasions and needs. Each of them can help you to cross the bridge to an ethical life filled with mitzvot.

4. Synagogue Prayers

Selected prayers with explanatory notes that provide background information and help you develop a familiarity with the format of synagogue prayers and rituals. Prayer is the bridge between you and God. For a good life you chart a course within the commandments. In ceremonies you celebrate God's wonders, and in prayer you attempt to establish a relationship with that unknown power.

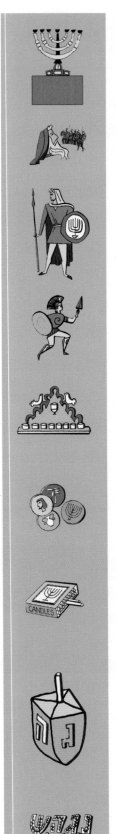

5. Hebrew Word Bank

Each of the sixteen "Why Holidays" and "Let's Celebrate" units is supplemented with a Hebrew Word Bank. The basic Hebrew words are integrated into the text. Hebrew terminology is one of the chief vehicles to transmit Jewish know-how and to speak in terms rooted in the religious tradition. The common bond through language is a unifying Jewish factor. A Hebrew vocabulary provides life-giving root to your Jewish family tree.

6. It's a Mitzvah

The text contains eighteen mitzvah units. The Torah tells us that humankind was created in the image of God. As a human you are challenged to copy the ethical qualities we ascribe to God. The Talmud tells us, "You can be like God. Just as God is merciful and charitable, so you too can be charitable and merciful."

Moses Maimonides identified 613 mitzvot in the Torah. The mitzvot are the qualities, that can inspire you to become a better and more ethical person.

I hope that **Holidays and Prayers** will enrich your lives and give you an appreciation of your Jewish Heritage.

Now start your mental engines and let's get to work.

WHY MITZVOT?

מִצְווֹת make Jewish life special. The word מִצְוָה means "commandment." According to Moses Maimonides, a great Jewish philosopher, there are תַּרְיַ"ג מִצְווֹת in the Torah. The Hebrew letters whose numerical value equals 613 spell the word תַּרְיַ"ג, so we call these the תַּרְיַ"ג מִצְווֹת.

There are מִצְווֹת עֲשֵׂה. These are mitzvot that God wants us to do, such as praying and honoring our parents.

There are מִצְווֹת that are the don't-do kind. These are called מִצְווֹת לֹא תַעֲשֶׂה. Don't steal and don't kill are just two examples.

There are מִצְווֹת associated with every part of your life: how you behave in school, how you play sports, how you treat your friends and family. מִצְווֹת are a part of the cycle of your Jewish life: birth, Bar Mitzvah/Bat Mitzvah, marriage, and death.

There are מִצְווֹת about the food you eat and how you will act as a grown-up in business or in your profession.

One מִצְוָה leads to another. For example, when you help someone, you may feel so good inside that before you know it you find yourself helping someone else! Or when your family has a Passover seder, they may also do the מִצְוָה of inviting a guest to share the holiday with them. The more מִצְווֹת you do, the more you will be following God's will, and you will be happier for it.

According to Maimonides, there are 613 mitzvot in the Torah. The Hebrew letters whose numerical value equals 613 spell *taryag*.

Study is an important מִצְוָה . Parents and teachers used to give children honey on the day their studies began. This showed the children that the study of the תּוֹרָה is sweet and encouraged them to learn. Study is important because it helps us to learn God's will. When we study the תּוֹרָה , we learn more about מִצְווֹת that we can do.

בְּרְכַּת הַמָּזוֹן

We thank God by reciting בְּרָכוֹת before and after a meal, הַמּוֹצִיא before we eat and the בְּרְכַּת הַמָּזוֹן at the end of the meal. It is a mitzvah to share with others and help them. When we give צְדָקָה , we are sharing and helping. When we do something God wants us to do we are good and we feel good. There are many more מִצְווֹת that remind us to appreciate all the good things that are a part of our lives.

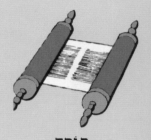

תּוֹרָה

Tzedakah

The Hebrew word צְדָקָה is sometimes translated as "charity," but it really means "righteousness," or doing the right thing. The Jewish idea of צְדָקָה goes much further than the idea of charity. In the Jewish view, it is not enough merely to help someone in need. It is also important to help in the kindest way possible, so as to protect the feelings of the person being helped. Best of all, you should help in such a way that the person can become self-supporting and no longer need charity. By making the recipient of charity independent you perform the מִצְוָה of restoring his or her human dignity. Moses Maimonides, one of the greatest Jewish thinkers, illustrated this point by listing a series of levels of צְדָקָה . All of the levels are good, because all represent ways of helping people in need, but some levels are better than others.

בְּרָכָה

הַמּוֹצִיא

The Seven Rabbinical Mitzvot

In addition to the תַּרְיַ"ג מִצְווֹת enumerated in the תּוֹרָה , the ancient sages established seven additional mitzvot, known as the מִצְווֹת דְרַבָּנָן the Rabbinical Mitzvot. These מִצְווֹת reflect religious and historical events that occurred after the giving of the תּוֹרָה .

צְדָקָה

MITZVOT AT HOME

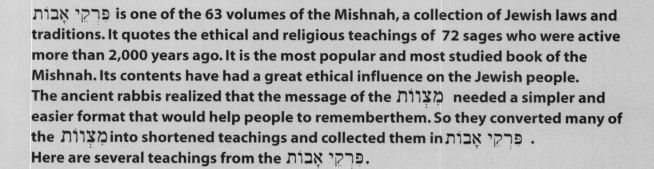

פִּרְקֵי אָבוֹת
ETHICS OF THE FATHERS

פִּרְקֵי אָבוֹת is one of the 63 volumes of the Mishnah, a collection of Jewish laws and traditions. It quotes the ethical and religious teachings of 72 sages who were active more than 2,000 years ago. It is the most popular and most studied book of the Mishnah. Its contents have had a great ethical influence on the Jewish people. The ancient rabbis realized that the message of the מִצְווֹת needed a simpler and easier format that would help people to remember them. So they converted many of the מִצְווֹת into shortened teachings and collected them in פִּרְקֵי אָבוֹת. Here are several teachings from the פִּרְקֵי אָבוֹת.

בֶּן־זוֹמָא אוֹמֵר:	Ben Zoma said:
״אֵיזֶהוּ חָכָם,	"Who is wise?
הַלוֹמֵד מִכָּל־אָדָם.	The person who learns from everyone else.
אֵיזֶהוּ גִבּוֹר?	Who is strong?
הַכּוֹבֵשׁ אֶת־יִצְרוֹ.	The person who controls his desires.
אֵיזֶהוּ עָשִׁיר?	Who is rich?
הַשָּׂמֵחַ בְּחֶלְקוֹ.	The person who is happy with what he has.
אֵיזֶהוּ מְכֻבָּד?	Who is honored?
הַמְכַבֵּד אֶת־הַבְּרִיּוֹת.״	The person who respects all creatures."

[Avot 4:1]

It's a Mitzvah 479

כִּי־פָתֹחַ תִּפְתַּח אֶת־יָדְךָ לוֹ
וְהַעֲבֵט תַּעֲבִיטֶנּוּ דֵּי מַחְסֹרוֹ
אֲשֶׁר יֶחְסַר לוֹ.

Let your hands be open and lend him generously whatever he needs.

(Devarim 15:8)

The Torah tells us that it is a מִצְוָה to give charity. Our sages said that the proper way to fulfill the מִצְוָה is to give one-tenth of one's earnings or profits. The תּוֹרָה refers to the ten percent as מַעֲשֵׂר. The Hebrew word מַעֲשֵׂר comes from the word עֶשֶׂר, meaning "ten."

In biblical times, the farmer would bring one-tenth of his produce to the Temple in Jerusalem to be divided among the Kohanim (priests), the Levites, and the poor. Today we give מַעֲשֵׂר in the form of money.

MITZVOT AT HOME

Wisdom quotes from פִּרְקֵי אָבוֹת

ON WHAT THE WORLD DEPENDS

שִׁמְעוֹן הַצַּדִּיק הָיָה
מִשְׁיָרֵי כְּנֶסֶת הַגְּדוֹלָה.
הוּא הָיָה אוֹמֵר,
"עַל-שְׁלֹשָׁה דְבָרִים הָעוֹלָם עוֹמֵד
עַל הַתּוֹרָה, וְעַל הָעֲבוֹדָה,
וְעַל גְּמִילוּת חֲסָדִים."

Shimon the Just was one of the
last survivors of the Great Assembly.
He used to say:
"The world depends on three things—
on Torah, on divine service,
and on charitable deeds."

Avot 1:2

WHO ARE YOU ?

אַרְבַּע מִדּוֹת בְּתַלְמִידִים:
מַהֵר לִשְׁמוֹעַ וּמַהֵר לְאַבֵּד –
קָשֶׁה לִשְׁמוֹעַ וְקָשֶׁה לְאַבֵּד –
מַהֵר לִשְׁמוֹעַ וְקָשֶׁה לְאַבֵּד –
קָשֶׁה לִשְׁמוֹעַ וּמַהֵר לְאַבֵּד –

There are four types of students.
1. Quick to learn and quick to forget
2. Slow to learn and slow to forget
3. Quick to learn and slow to forget
4. Slow to learn and quick to forget

Avot 5:12

RESPECT

רַבִּי אֶלְעָזָר בֶּן שַׁמּוּעַ אוֹמֵר:
"יְהִי כְבוֹד תַּלְמִידָךְ
חָבִיב עָלֶיךָ כְּשֶׁלָּךְ,
וּכְבוֹד חֲבֵרָךְ
כְּמוֹרָא רַבָּךְ,
וּמוֹרָא רַבָּךְ
כְּמוֹרָא שָׁמַיִם".

Rabbi Elazar ben Shamua says:
"Let the welfare of your students
be as vital to you as your own.
And the welfare of your friends
be as vital as your respect for your teachers.
And your respect for your teachers
be as great as your respect for heaven."

Avot 4:12

RESPECT FOR THE POOR

יוֹסֵי בֶּן יוֹחָנָן, אִישׁ יְרוּשָׁלַיִם, אוֹמֵר:
"יְהִי בֵיתְךָ פָּתוּחַ לִרְוָחָה,
וְיִהְיוּ עֲנִיִּים
בְּנֵי בֵיתֶךָ".

Jose ben Yohanan from Jerusalem says:
"Let your house be open wide,
and let the poor be
members of your household."

Avot 1:5

11

THE HEBREW CALENDAR

The לוּחַ we use in our daily life is based upon the revolution of our planet around the שֶׁמֶשׁ. The Jewish לוּחַ is a lunar, or moon, calendar. It divides the time according to the cycles of the רֹאשׁ חֹדֶשׁ. Our ancient rabbis measured time by using the journey of the לְבָנָה around the earth as a basic לוּחַ unit.
They called 29–30 days, from full לְבָנָה to full לְבָנָה, is a חֹדֶשׁ.
Twelve full moons, or חֳדָשִׁים, are called a שָׁנָה. The ancients found out that the לְבָנָה year was not in sync with the sun year.
The moon חֳדָשִׁים could not keep up with the seasons. After a while, Rosh Hashanah would be in the spring instead of the autumn. Passover could end up in the winter instead of spring.
Jewish mathematicians found an answer.
They added an extra חֹדֶשׁ to certain years so that the לְבָנָה and the sun years were on the same track. These special years are called leap years. This adjustment made the חֳדָשִׁים of the Jewish calendar moon חֳדָשִׁים, and the year became a solar, or שֶׁמֶשׁ, year.

HEBREW WORD BANK

1	לוּחַ	Calendar
2	תִּשְׁרֵי	Seventh Hebrew month
3	חֹדֶשׁ, חֳדָשִׁים	Month, months
4	רֹאשׁ חֹדֶשׁ	New moon
5	לְבָנָה	Moon
6	סַנְהֶדְרִין	Religious court
7	שָׁנָה	Year
8	שֶׁמֶשׁ	Sun

When there is a leap year, the extra חֹדֶשׁ is added after Adar. The extra חֹדֶשׁ is called Adar Sheni, or Second Adar.

The Hebrew Months
The Hebrew names of the חֳדָשִׁים come from the Babylonian לוּחַ. Here are the Hebrew names for each of the חֳדָשִׁים and the Jewish holidays that are celebrated in that חֹדֶשׁ.

ASTROLOGICAL SYMBOLS FOR THE JEWISH MONTHS

חֶשְׁוָן CHESHVAN	אייר IYAR	סִיוָן SIVAN
תִּשְׁרֵי TISHREI	אב AV	נִיסָן NISAN
אֱלוּל ELUL	טֵבֵת TEVET	אֲדָר ADAR
תַּמּוּז TAMMUZ	שְׁבָט SHEVAT	כִּסְלֵו KISLEV

תִּשְׁרֵי Tishrei – Rosh Hashanah, Yom Kippur, Sukkot, Simchat Torah

חֶשְׁוָן Cheshvan

כִּסְלֵו Kislev – Chanukah

טֵבֵת Tevet

שְׁבָט Shevat – Tu Bishevat

אֲדָר Adar – Purim

נִיסָן Nisan – Passover, Yom Hashoah

אִיָּיר Iyar – Yom Ha-Zikaron, Yom Ha-Atzma'ut, Lag B'Omer

סִיוָן Sivan – Shavuot

תַּמּוּז Tammuz

אָב Av – Tishah Be-Av

אֱלוּל Elul

ראש חדש

But what did people do before there was a printed לוּחַ?
How did they manage without a לוּחַ?
The shepherds of ancient Palestine were filled with wonder by
the לְבָנָה changes. They had no lamps, so they went to bed at
sunset and got up at sunrise. Men, women, and children thought
of the שֶׁמֶשׁ as a wonderful friend.

לוּחַ

Report to the Sanhedrin

Special observers were placed at stations to wait for the
appearance of the new ראש חדש. As soon at the slightest crescent
showed in the sky the observers rushed to Jerusalem. They
rushed to the סַנְהֶדְרִין, the High Court of the Jewish people.
"We testify that we have seen the new ראש חדש," they swore.
They reported the exact moment it made its appearance.
Then the סַנְהֶדְרִין officially proclaimed the new ראש חדש, and
runners were sent to light fires on the mountaintops surrounding
Jerusalem.
As soon as the signals were seen by the inhabitants of other
towns, they lit their own fire. In a short time the signals reached
all the towns in Israel. Thus ראש חדש was officially begun.

שֶׁמֶשׁ

לְבָנָה

WHY ROSH CHODESH?

HEBREW WORD BANK

Long ago, in the time of the First בֵּית־הַמִּקְדָּשׁ, the beginning of the רֹאשׁ חֹדֶשׁ was celebrated with great festivity. The שׁוֹפָר was blown. People did not go to work. They went to יְרוּשָׁלַיִם. There they sacrificed a special רֹאשׁ חֹדֶשׁ offering and then held a family feast. Many of these customs could no longer be practiced after the בֵּית־הַמִּקְדָּשׁ was destroyed. But other customs developed. Special prayers were said in honor of the רֹאשׁ חֹדֶשׁ. One of the prayers was הַלֵּל.

It is a special prayer of praise to God that is recited only on holidays. But an exception is made for רֹאשׁ חֹדֶשׁ, when half-הַלֵּל is recited.

חֹדֶשׁ, חֲדָשִׁים	1 Month, months
רֹאשׁ חֹדֶשׁ	2 Beginning of the month
קִדּוּשׁ לְבָנָה	3 Blessing of a New Moon
בֵּית־הַמִּקְדָּשׁ	4 Holy Temple
שׁוֹפָר	5 Ram's horn
הַלֵּל	6 Prayer of praise
יְרוּשָׁלַיִם	7 Jerusalem
לְבָנָה	8 Moon

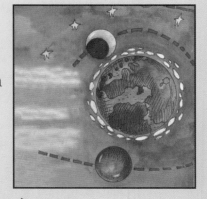

The New Moon

Jews also observe the custom of blessing the new moon- קִדּוּשׁ לְבָנָה. In this ancient ceremony Jews gather in groups outdoors. When the לְבָנָה is visible to all each says to his neighbor: "Blessed be the Almighty, who renews the חֹדֶשׁ. Shalom Aleichem!" and everyone replies: "Peace be to you. May this חֹדֶשׁ bring *mazal* (good fortune) to us and to all mankind!"

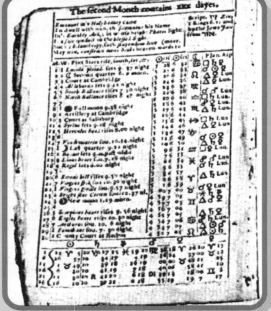

A calendar based on the Bible was introduced by the Pilgrims in Massachusetts in 1666. The Pilgrims studied and revered the Bible. They used the Hebrew names of the months in this early American calendar.

Two-Day Holidays

Most Reform Jews celebrate the holidays of the Jewish year for one day, the same as some of the ancient Jews did in the time of the Bible. Orthodox and Conservative Jews, celebrate the holidays for two days.

Long ago, the Jews lived in the Land of Israel. At that time, they observed each holiday for only one day. They did not have written calendars as we do today.

The Jews who remained in Israel, of course, continued to celebrate the holidays for only one day. Nowadays we have written calendars that tell us exactly when the new moon appears, even though we may not see it ourselves. Thus we always know when a new חֹדֶשׁ begins, and we always know the dates of the holidays.

Since we no longer have the problem Reform Jews decided to observe the holidays for only one day.

בֵּית־הַמִּקְדָּשׁ

שׁוֹפָר

יְרוּשָׁלַיִם

לְבָנָה

It's a Mitzvah 4

הַחֹדֶשׁ הַזֶּה לָכֶם
רֹאשׁ חֳדָשִׁים

This month shall be for you the beginning of months.

Shemot 12:2

Before the invention of the calendar, it was a mitzvah for the Sanhedrin in יְרוּשָׁלַיִם to certify the רֹאשׁ חֹדֶשׁ on the testimony of two reliable witnesses who had seen the רֹאשׁ חֹדֶשׁ. This declaration sets the dates of all the holidays.

The proclamation of the רֹאשׁ חֹדֶשׁ was signaled from mountaintop to mountaintop by beacon fires. Today the beginning of each רֹאשׁ חֹדֶשׁ is announced in the synagogue and special prayers are recited. You can do a mitzvah by attending רֹאשׁ חֹדֶשׁ services. In the רֹאשׁ חֹדֶשׁ prayer we ask Adonai to make the new חֹדֶשׁ a time of happiness, joy, and gladness. We also ask Adonai to pardon and forgive our sins.

ROSH CHODESH IN THE SYNAGOGUE

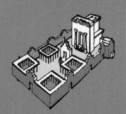

בִּרְכַּת הַחֹדֶשׁ
BLESSING FOR THE NEW MONTH

This prayer is recited in the synagogue when the arrival of a new month is announced.

יְהִי רָצוֹן מִלְּפָנֶיךָ,	May it be Your will,
יְיָ אֱלֹהֵינוּ,	O God,
וֵאלֹהֵי אֲבוֹתֵינוּ,	who is the God of our ancestors,
שֶׁתְּחַדֵּשׁ עָלֵינוּ	To renew for us
אֶת הַחֹדֶשׁ הַזֶּה	This coming month
לְטוֹבָה וְלִבְרָכָה.	For good things and blessings.
יְחַדְּשֵׁהוּ הַקָּדוֹשׁ בָּרוּךְ הוּא	May the Holy One renew
עָלֵינוּ	us His people
וְעַל כָּל עַמּוֹ בֵּית יִשְׂרָאֵל	and the house of Israel,
לְחַיִּים וּלְשָׁלוֹם,	With life and with peace,
לְשָׂשׂוֹן וּלְשִׂמְחָה,	With gladness and with joy,
לִישׁוּעָה וּלְנֶחָמָה,	With His help and loving care,
וְנֹאמַר אָמֵן:	And let us say, Amen.

סֵדֶר הַלֵּל
THE HALLEL SERVICE

The Book of Tehillim consists of 150 psalms composed by King David. Many of the psalms are found in the Siddur and the Machzor. The הַלֵּל prayers consist of Psalms 113–118. It is a rabbinical mitzvah to recite the half–הַלֵּל (Psalms 115–116) on every רֹאשׁ חֹדֶשׁ and on certain days of Passover.

The הַלֵּל service starts with this blessing.

בָּרוּךְ אַתָּה יְיָ,	Praised are you, Adonai,
אֱלֹהֵינוּ מֶלֶךְ הָעוֹלָם,	Our God, Ruler of the universe,
אֲשֶׁר קִדְּשָׁנוּ בְּמִצְוֹתָיו	Who has made us holy with commandments
וְצִוָּנוּ	And instructed us
לִקְרֹא אֶת הַהַלֵּל.	To recite the Hallel.

ROSH CHODESH IN THE SYNAGOGUE

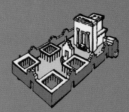

הַלֵּל
PSALMS OF PRAISE

The הַלֵּל psalms are songs of joy and happiness that have accompanied our people on their journey through history. They have strengthened us in times of sorrow and given us happiness in times of joy.

On רֹאשׁ חֹדֶשׁ we recite half הַלֵּל, which consist of Psalms 115 and 116.

יְיָ זְכָרָנוּ, יְבָרֵךְ,	Adonai will remember and bless us,
יְבָרֵךְ אֶת־בֵּית יִשְׂרָאֵל,	Adonai will bless the house of Israel,
יְבָרֵךְ אֶת־בֵּית אַהֲרֹן.	Adonai will bless the house of Aaron.
יְבָרֵךְ יִרְאֵי יְיָ,	Those who respect Adonai will be blessed,
הַקְּטַנִּים עִם־הַגְּדֹלִים.	Both children and adults.
יֹסֵף יְיָ עֲלֵיכֶם,	May Adonai make your family fruitful,
עֲלֵיכֶם וְעַל־בְּנֵיכֶם,	You and your children,
בְּרוּכִים אַתֶּם לַיְיָ,	Because you are blessed by Adonai,
עֹשֵׂה שָׁמַיִם וָאָרֶץ.	Who created the cosmos and the planet earth.
הַשָּׁמַיִם שָׁמַיִם לַיְיָ,	The cosmos was created by Adonai,
וְהָאָרֶץ נָתַן לִבְנֵי־אָדָם.	And the earth was given to the human race.
לֹא־הַמֵּתִים יְהַלְלוּ־יָהּ	The dead are silent
וְלֹא כָּל־יֹרְדֵי דוּמָה.	And cannot praise Adonai.
וַאֲנַחְנוּ נְבָרֵךְ יָהּ	But we will praise Adonai
מֵעַתָּה וְעַד־עוֹלָם.	From now and forever.
הַלְלוּיָהּ.	Halleluyah – Praise Adonai.

Psalm 115:12–18

WHY ROSH HASHANAH?

An autumn chill is in the air, and the lemony greens of summer have changed to the russets, cinnamons, and burnished browns of leaves that crackle underfoot.

People who crowded the beaches during the summer have changed to more formal clothes and returned to their offices and schools.

And the children are back in class, with shiny new notebooks, sharpened pencils, and full hearts. Autumn is a time of changes and beginnings.

But the most important change of autumn does not have to do with the weather. For Jewish people autumn marks the holiest time of the year—the עֲשֶׂרֶת יְמֵי תְּשׁוּבָה —a time of inner change.

During this season, Jews remember the promises they made to God, to one another, and to themselves. They remember their promises to observe the laws of Torah. They ask themselves thoughtfully whether they have fulfilled their promises.

They proudly remember their good deeds, and sadly, too, they recall their dishonesties, their sins, their acts of cruelty, great and small. They pray to God for forgiveness, and they struggle to change inside and become better people.

The holidays of this solemn season are רֹאשׁ הַשָׁנָה and יוֹם כִּפּוּר. The ten days between these two holidays are called the עֲשֶׂרֶת יְמֵי תְּשׁוּבָה.

A father–and–son combination: Bernard Scharfstein reads the notes, and Asher Scharfstein blows the shofar.

HEBREW WORD BANK

1	רֹאשׁ הַשָׁנָה	The New Year
2	תִּשְׁרֵי	The month of Tishrei
3	עֲשֶׂרֶת יְמֵי תְּשׁוּבָה	Ten Days of Repentance
4	יוֹם כִּפּוּר	Day of Atonement
5	שַׁבַּת שׁוּבָה	Sabbath of Return
6	שׁוֹפָר	Ram's horn
7	תּוֹרָה, תּוֹרוֹת	Torah, Torahs
8	בֵּית הַכְּנֶסֶת	Synagogue

ROSH HASHANAH

שׁוֹפָר

Shabbat Shuvah

The Sabbath that occurs between רֹאשׁ הַשָּׁנָה and יוֹם כִּפּוּר is called שַׁבָּת שׁוּבָה—the Sabbath of Return.

On this day, Jews feel a deep and special yearning to return to God and Torah. On שַׁבָּת שׁוּבָה, we promise God that we will do our best to become better Jews.

תּוֹרָה

Did You Know?

יהוה ADONAI

The prayers in the Siddur, Bible, and Machzor use several names for God.

God's special holy name, Adonai, was first revealed to Moses at the meeting with God at the burning bush. Moses was shepherding the flock of his father-in-law, Jethro, in the desert of Sinai. Suddenly he spied a bush that was aflame, but the bush itself was not consumed by fire. Adonai called to Moses from the midst of the burning bush and said, "Take off your shoes, for the place on which you are standing is holy ground."

God continued and said, "Tell the Children of Israel, that Adonai, the God of your ancestors, spoke to you. This is my name for ever and ever."

God's special divine name is written with four Hebrew letters, יהוה, and is pronounced Adonai. Some non-Jewish scholars pronounce it Yahweh.

It is clear that the four-letter tetragrammaton comes from the Hebrew word הָיָה "to be." It means that God was, God is, and God will be forever.

The secret pronunciation of the name was passed on to Aaron, who passed it on to the High Priest. Whenever the four-letter tetragrammaton יהוה is found in the Bible or Siddur, it is pronounced Adonai. In the Siddur and Machzor יהוה is sometimes written as יְיָ.

תִּשְׁרֵי

בֵּית הַכְּנֶסֶת

LET'S CELEBRATE ROSH HASHANAH

רֹאשׁ הַשָּׁנָה, the Jewish New Year,
is a serious time of prayer, thoughtfulness,
and inner change.
רֹאשׁ הַשָּׁנָה is celebrated each year,
in Israel and the world over, on the first
two days of the month of תִּשְׁרֵי.

Selichot
On the Saturday night before
רֹאשׁ הַשָּׁנָה, after the clock has struck
twelve and the world has become very
quiet, Jews the world over go to the
temple to say סְלִיחוֹת.
We are in a very grave mood,
for this is a time to recite
special prayers of repentance and to
ask for forgiveness.
Some of the prayers are
beautiful poems composed by Jewish
scholars and poets. They recall the hardships of exile, persecution,
and martyrdom which our people have endured. סְלִיחוֹת are
also said during the rest of the עֲשֶׂרֶת יְמֵי תְּשׁוּבָה.
When we recite סְלִיחוֹת, we ask God to forgive our sins
and to send help when humankind needs it most.

HEBREW WORD BANK

1 רֹאשׁ הַשָּׁנָה	The New Year
2 יוֹם תְּרוּעָה	Day of shofar blowing
3 דְּבַשׁ	Honey
4 מַחְזוֹר	Prayerbook for High Holy Days
5 יוֹם הַזִּכָּרוֹן	The Day of Remembering
6 תְּקִיעָה	Shofar note–1 blast
7 שְׁבָרִים	Shofar note–3 short blasts
8 תְּרוּעָה	Shofar note–9 short blasts
9 תַּשְׁלִיךְ	Ceremony of casting away sins
10 יָמִים נוֹרָאִים	Days of Awe
11 וּנְתַנֶּה תֹּקֶף	Rosh Hashanah prayer

A New Year greeting card

The Machzor
The weekday and Sabbath prayerbook is called a Siddur.
The festival prayerbook is called a מַחְזוֹר.
The word מַחְזוֹר comes from the word chazor, meaning
"cycle." There is a מַחְזוֹר with prayers for each main
Jewish holiday: Rosh Hashanah, Yom Kippur, Sukkot,
Passover, and Shavuot.

20

The Meaning of Rosh Hashanah

On רֹאשׁ הַשָּׁנָה Jews try to remember every detail about their behavior over the past year. "Was I as honest, as helpful, as loving as I might have been?" they ask themselves. They judge themselves strictly, and they try to become better Jews. Another Hebrew name for רֹאשׁ הַשָּׁנָה is יוֹם הַזִּכָּרוֹן, the Day of Remembering.

יוֹם תְּרוּעָה

The Shofar

At the synagogue on רֹאשׁ הַשָּׁנָה the cantor sings traditional, beautiful melodies as well as some by modern composers. The clear, resonant voice of the שׁוֹפָר is sounded many times. All over the world, it calls Jews to return to Torah, to inner change. The voice of the שׁוֹפָר is such an important part of the holiday that רֹאשׁ הַשָּׁנָה is sometimes called יוֹם תְּרוּעָה. Many people gather near Jerusalem's Western Wall to hear the שׁוֹפָר call.

שׁוֹפָר

The Meaning of the Shofar's Call

In biblical times the שׁוֹפָר was used to herald great moments.
It proclaimed the ascent of a new king upon the throne; it announced the Jubilee every fiftieth year and the beginning of Sabbaths and festivals. In wartime it signaled the army to battle.

The שׁוֹפָר has so long been associated with Jewish tradition that it has become a holy symbol. It recalls the offering of Isaac by Abraham, for on that occasion God, recognizing our people's devotion, ordered Abraham to substitute a ram for his son as a sacrifice on the altar.

It reminds us of the giving of the Ten Commandments to the accompaniment of שׁוֹפָר blasts on Mount Sinai.

תַּפּוֹחַ וּדְבַשׁ

Before the שׁוֹפָר is blown we recite Psalm 37, which says that the שׁוֹפָר will one day announce God's dominion over all peoples. Then the horn is sounded. There are three variations in the call: תְּקִיעָה, שְׁבָרִים, and תְּרוּעָה.
תְּקִיעָה is a long blast starting on a low note and rising nearly an octave; שְׁבָרִים consists of three shorter notes; תְּרוּעָה is made up of nine quick, sharp calls ending with a high note.

מַחֲזוֹר

The Prayer Called Unetaneh Tokef

One of the most important prayers read on רֹאשׁ הַשָּׁנָה and also recited on Yom Kippur is וּנְתַנֶּה תֹּקֶף. It was composed by Rabbi Amnon of Mayence. The local bishop repeatedly urged him to leave his faith and convert to Christianity, but he always refused. Once, instead of refusing immediately, he requested a period of three days in which to think about it.

When alone, he felt so guilty for not having simply said no that when he was called to the bishop he asked that his tongue be cut out. Instead, the bishop had the rabbi's hands and feet amputated. In this condition, Rabbi Amnon was carried to the synagogue for the רֹאשׁ הַשָּׁנָה services. As the cantor and congregation were about to begin the Kedushah, the sanctification service, Rabbi Amnon asked permission to offer a prayer he had composed. As soon as the last word had left his lips, the rabbi's life mercifully ended. וּנְתַנֶּה תֹּקֶף expresses the idea of holiness and awe which fills the רֹאשׁ הַשָּׁנָה service. It says, in part:

> We will celebrate the mighty holiness of this day, a day of awe and terror. . . . You open the Book of Records . . . a great trumpet is sounded, and a still, small voice is heard. . . . The angels proclaim: This is the day of judgment and all who enter the world You cause to pass before You like a flock of sheep.

Rosh Hashanah Greetings and Foods

Jews greet one another during this season with the blessing, "May you be written down for a good year." During this time, according to tradition, God writes down all our names and decides what the coming year will bring for us. Hoping for a sweet new year, Jews traditionally eat sweet foods on רֹאשׁ הַשָּׁנָה. We dip apples and challah into דְּבָשׁ. All over Israel and the world, Jews eat tsimmis—a mixture of carrots, meat, and דְּבָשׁ—and tayglach—cake in a candy-like דְּבָשׁ coating

Tashlich

Jews group together on רֹאשׁ הַשָׁנָה for the תַּשְׁלִיךְ custom. Throwing small pieces of bread into a stream of running water, they say a special prayer. They pray that as the running water carries away the bread, so too will their own sins be carried away and forgiven by God. Many Israelis observe the תַּשְׁלִיךְ custom along the waters of the Mediterranean Sea or Lake Kinneret.

יוֹם תְּרוּעָה

At Home

After services, the family gathers for a festive meal. First, the blessing over wine is recited, then a family member says Ha-Motzi over the challah. Often the challot are baked in the shape of a ladder or a bird. The ladder symbolizes the wish that our prayers may go upward and be heard by the Almighty. The bird is a symbol of mercy, for God has mercy even upon birds.

שׁוֹפָר

  **Did You Know?**

תַּפּוּחַ וּדְבַשׁ

SERVICE OF THE HEART עֲבוֹדַת הַלֵּב

When the Romans in 70 B.C.E. destroyed the Second Temple, the temple service was replaced by the synagogue service. Unlike the temple, priests, Levites, and sacrifices were unimportant for the religious mission of the synagogue service. Now, the emphasis was on the people and their prayers as a means of communication with the Almighty. The synagogue now became a portable temple, which could be transported wherever Jews decided to live or were forced to settle. New prayers and ceremonies were introduced and the temple service and pageantry were replaced by the עֲבוֹדַת הַלֵּב. Our sages taught that the essence of Torah was to love Adonai with all your heart and with all your soul. They felt that without heartfelt deeds to match them, prayers were just formalized words. As they are spoken, they need to be alive and true. When prayers are true and penetrating, they forge a permanent bond with the Almighty. Prayer is the עֲבוֹדַת הַלֵּב. Put your heart into your words and deeds.

מַחֲזוֹר

הַדְלָקַת נֵרוֹת לְרֹאשׁ הַשָׁנָה
CANDLE LIGHTING FOR ROSH HASHANAH

A blessing is thank you for a gift from Adonai. When we light רֹאשׁ הַשָׁנָה candles we are thanking Adonai for the gift of light, without which there would be no life, and for bringing us to this happy time of year.

בָּרוּךְ אַתָּה יְיָ,   Praised is Adonai

אֱלֹהֵינוּ מֶלֶךְ הָעוֹלָם,   our God, Ruler of the universe,

אֲשֶׁר קִדְּשָׁנוּ בְּמִצְוֹתָיו   who made us holy by the mitzvot

וְצִוָּנוּ לְהַדְלִיק נֵר שֶׁל יוֹם טוֹב.   by commanding us to light candles on the festival.

בָּרוּךְ אַתָּה יְיָ,   Praised is Adonai,

אֱלֹהֵינוּ מֶלֶךְ הָעוֹלָם,   our God, Ruler of the universe,

שֶׁהֶחֱיָנוּ וְקִיְּמָנוּ   who has kept us alive and well

וְהִגִּיעָנוּ לַזְּמַן הַזֶּה.   and has given us the opportunity to celebrate this occasion.

Did You Know?

The holiday of רֹאשׁ הַשָׁנָה is also known as יוֹם הַזִכָּרוֹן.
On יוֹם הַזִכָּרוֹן there are many things to remember. You pray to Adonai :"Remember us to life". We also pray to be remembered for our good deeds.
The Kiddush on page 25 calls רֹאשׁ הַשָׁנָה a יוֹם הַזִכָּרוֹן.

ROSH HASHANAH AT HOME

קִדּוּשׁ לְרֹאשׁ הַשָּׁנָה

KIDDUSH FOR ROSH HASHANAH

The Kiddush of רֹאשׁ הַשָּׁנָה highlights our Exodus from Egypt and the sounding of the שׁוֹפָר. The Kiddush also calls רֹאשׁ הַשָּׁנָה , יוֹם הַזִּכָּרוֹן and יוֹם תְּרוּעָה.

בָּרוּךְ אַתָּה יְיָ,	Praised are you Adonai our God,
אֱלֹהֵינוּ מֶלֶךְ הָעוֹלָם,	Ruler of the universe,
בּוֹרֵא פְּרִי הַגָּפֶן.	Creator of the fruit of the vine.

בָּרוּךְ אַתָּה יְהֹוָה אֱלֹהֵינוּ,	Praised are you Adonai our God,
מֶלֶךְ הָעוֹלָם,	Ruler of the universe,
אֲשֶׁר בָּחַר־בָּנוּ	who has chosen us from among all
מִכָּל־עָם	peoples
וְרוֹמְמָנוּ מִכָּל־לָשׁוֹן	and exalted us above all tongues [peoples]
וְקִדְּשָׁנוּ	and hallowed us
בְּמִצְוֹתָיו.	with His commandments.
וַתִּתֶּן־לָנוּ יְהֹוָה אֱלֹהֵינוּ,	Adonai our God, You have given us
בְּאַהֲבָה אֶת [יוֹם הַשַּׁבָּת הַזֶּה וְאֶת]	with love, this (Shabbat and this)
יוֹם הַזִּכָּרוֹן הַזֶּה,	Day of Remembrance,
יוֹם תְּרוּעָה	this day of sounding the shofar
[בְּאַהֲבָה] מִקְרָא קֹדֶשׁ	(with love), a holy occasion
זֵכֶר לִיצִיאַת מִצְרָיִם.	recalling the Exodus from Egypt.

כִּי בָנוּ בָחַרְתָּ וְאוֹתָנוּ קִדַּשְׁתָּ	You have chosen us and consecrated us
מִכָּל־הָעַמִּים.	from among all peoples.
וּדְבָרְךָ אֱמֶת וְקַיָּם לָעַד.	Your word is true, enduring forever.
בָּרוּךְ אַתָּה יְהֹוָה,	Praised are you Adonai,
מֶלֶךְ עַל כָּל־הָאָרֶץ,	Ruler of all the universe,
מְקַדֵּשׁ [הַשַּׁבָּת וְ]יִשְׂרָאֵל	who hallows (Shabbat and) Israel
וְיוֹם הַזִּכָּרוֹן.	and the Day of Remembrance.

ROSH HASHANAH IN THE SYNAGOGUE

| תְּקִיעַת הַשּׁוֹפָר SHOFAR BLESSINGS |

Before the sounding of the שׁוֹפָר we recite the following two blessings.

בָּרוּךְ אַתָּה יְיָ,
Praised is Adonai,

אֱלֹהֵינוּ מֶלֶךְ הָעוֹלָם,
our God, Ruler of the universe

אֲשֶׁר קִדְּשָׁנוּ בְּמִצְוֹתָיו
who has made us holy by the mitzvot

וְצִוָּנוּ לִשְׁמוֹעַ קוֹל שׁוֹפָר.
and commanded us to listen to the sound of the shofar.

בָּרוּךְ אַתָּה יְיָ,
Praised is Adonai,

אֱלֹהֵינוּ מֶלֶךְ הָעוֹלָם,
our God, Ruler of the universe,

שֶׁהֶחֱיָנוּ וְקִיְּמָנוּ
who kept us alive and well

וְהִגִּיעָנוּ לַזְּמַן הַזֶּה.
and has given the opportunity to celebrate this occasion.

THE SHOFAR NOTES

תְּקִיעָה שְׁבָרִים תְּרוּעָה תְּקִיעָה
תְּקִיעָה שְׁבָרִים תְּקִיעָה
תְּקִיעָה תְּרוּעָה תְּקִיעָה

| הַיּוֹם הֲרַת עוֹלָם |

The prayer הַיּוֹם הֲרַת עוֹלָם is repeated after each blowing of the שׁוֹפָר.
The prayer tells us that on this day the world was born and now the slate is wiped
clean. A רֹאשׁ הַשָּׁנָה has started, and our efforts must be directed to keeping it clean.

הַיּוֹם הֲרַת עוֹלָם.
Today the world is newborn.

הַיּוֹם יַעֲמִיד בַּמִּשְׁפָּט
Today we stand to be judged.

כָּל־יְצוּרֵי עוֹלָמִים
We, all Your creatures,

אִם כְּבָנִים אִם כַּעֲבָדִים.
Some as children, some as servants,

אִם כְּבָנִים
As children

רַחֲמֵנוּ כְּרַחֵם אָב עַל בָּנִים.
Have mercy! Just as a parent of children.

וְאִם כַּעֲבָדִים
As servants

עֵינֵינוּ לְךָ תְלוּיוֹת
We prayerfully look toward You.

עַד שֶׁתְּחָנֵּנוּ
Decide to give us life

וְתוֹצִיא כָאוֹר מִשְׁפָּטֵנוּ.
When You decide our fate.

אָיֹם קָדוֹשׁ.
You are an awesome, holy God.

26

סֵפֶר הַחַיִּים **THE BOOK OF LIFE**

These are the Days of Judgment. Tradition tells us that during this period the Book of Life is opened. In this prayer we ask Adonai to remember us for a life of peace and prosperity.

זָכְרֵנוּ לְחַיִּים,	Remember us for life,
מֶלֶךְ חָפֵץ בַּחַיִּים,	O Ruler who wants to give life,
וְכָתְבֵנוּ בְּסֵפֶר הַחַיִּים,	and inscribe us in the Book of Life,
לְמַעַנְךָ אֱלֹהִים חַיִּים.	for Your sake, God of life.
מִי כָמוֹךָ אַב הָרַחֲמִים	Who can be compared to You, Merciful One?
זוֹכֵר יְצוּרָיו לַחַיִּים בְּרַחֲמִים:	In mercy You remember Your creatures with life.

• כָּתְבֵנוּ בְּסֵפֶר הַחַיִּים is a celebration of life. This theme is found in the prayer רֹאשׁ הַשָּׁנָה

בְּסֵפֶר חַיִּים בְּרָכָה וְשָׁלוֹם	In the book of life, blessing, peace,
וּפַרְנָסָה טוֹבָה	and prosperity
נִזָּכֵר וְנִכָּתֵם	may we be remembered and inscribed
לְפָנֶיךָ,	before You,
אֲנַחְנוּ וְכָל־עַמְּךָ	we and all Your people
בֵּית יִשְׂרָאֵל,	the house of Israel,
לְחַיִּים טוֹבִים וּלְשָׁלוֹם.	for a good life and for peace.
בָּרוּךְ אַתָּה יְיָ,	Praised are You, Adonai,
עוֹשֶׂה הַשָּׁלוֹם.	who makes peace.

 # Did You Know?

The traditional greeting for רֹאשׁ הַשָּׁנָה *is:*
לְשָׁנָה טוֹבָה תִּכָּתֵבוּ
"May you be inscribed for a good year."
A good year means a year of peace, a year of health, a year of happy family life, and a year filled with mitzvot and good deeds.

אָבִינוּ מַלְכֵּנוּ
OUR PARENT, OUR RULER

The Torah tells us that Adonai created the universe and that all of humanity are children of Adonai. Adonai is אָבִינוּ מַלְכֵּינוּ. The יָמִים נוֹרָאִים, Rosh Hashanah and Yom Kippur, remind us that we are not alone. אָבִינוּ מַלְכֵּינוּ is always with us.

אָבִינוּ מַלְכֵּינוּ, אֵין לָנוּ מֶלֶךְ אֶלָּא אָתָּה.
Our Parent, our Ruler, we have no Ruler other than You.

אָבִינוּ מַלְכֵּינוּ, עֲשֵׂה עִמָּנוּ לְמַעַן שְׁמֶךָ.
Our Parent, our Ruler, help us for Your own sake.

אָבִינוּ מַלְכֵּנוּ, חַדֵּשׁ עָלֵינוּ שָׁנָה טוֹבָה.
Our Parent, our Ruler, grant us a good new year.

אָבִינוּ מַלְכֵּינוּ, סְלַח וּמְחַל לְכָל־עֲווֹנוֹתֵינוּ.
Our Parent, our Ruler, forgive and pardon all our sins.

אָבִינוּ מַלְכֵּינוּ, הַחֲזִירֵנוּ בִּתְשׁוּבָה שְׁלֵמָה לְפָנֶיךָ.
Our Parent, our Ruler, help us return with complete repentance to You.

אָבִינוּ מַלְכֵּינוּ, כָּתְבֵנוּ בְּסֵפֶר חַיִּים טוֹבִים:
Our Parent, our Ruler, inscribe us in the book of good life.

? Did You Know?

A GOOD AND SWEET YEAR

The ancient sages were ahead of their times. They knew that symbols and ceremonies have the ability to convey messages. After Kiddush we dip a piece of challah into דְּבַשׁ. After eating the challah, we also dip a piece of apple into דְּבַשׁ and recite:

יְהִי רָצוֹן מִלְפָנֶיךָ,
May it be Your will,

יְיָ אֱלֹהֵינוּ
our God

וֵאלֹהֵי אֲבוֹתֵינוּ,
and God of our ancestors,

שֶׁתְּחַדֵּשׁ עָלֵינוּ
to renew for us

שָׁנָה טוֹבָה וּמְתוּקָה:
a good and sweet year.

אָנוּ עַמֶּךְ **WE ARE YOUR PEOPLE**

This prayer is the introduction to the two confessions (see page 36). The prayer describes the parallel relationship between Israel and Adonai.

אֱלֹהֵינוּ וֵאלֹהֵי אֲבוֹתֵינוּ,	Our God and God of our ancestors,
סְלַח לָנוּ, מְחַל לָנוּ, כַּפֶּר־לָנוּ.	Forgive us, pardon us, and atone for us.
כִּי אָנוּ עַמֶּךְ וְאַתָּה אֱלֹהֵינוּ,	We are Your people and You are our God,
אָנוּ בָנֶיךָ וְאַתָּה אָבִינוּ.	We are Your children and You are our parent.
אָנוּ עֲבָדֶיךָ וְאַתָּה אֲדוֹנֵנוּ,	We are Your servants and You are our master,
אָנוּ קְהָלֶךָ וְאַתָּה חֶלְקֵנוּ.	We are Your congregation and You are our leader.
אָנוּ נַחֲלָתֶךָ וְאַתָּה גוֹרָלֵנוּ,	We are Your heritage and You are our destiny,
אָנוּ צֹאנֶךָ וְאַתָּה רוֹעֵנוּ.	We are Your sheep and You are our shepherd.
אָנוּ כַרְמֶךָ וְאַתָּה נוֹטְרֵנוּ,	We are Your vineyards and You are our watchman,
אָנוּ פְעֻלָּתֶךָ וְאַתָּה יוֹצְרֵנוּ.	We are Your creations and You are our creator.
אָנוּ רַעְיָתֶךָ וְאַתָּה דוֹדֵנוּ,	We are Your faithful and You are beloved,
אָנוּ סְגֻלָּתֶךָ וְאַתָּה קְרוֹבֵנוּ.	We are Your treasure and You are our protector.
אָנוּ עַמֶּךָ וְאַתָּה מַלְכֵּנוּ,	We are Your subjects and You are our ruler,
אָנוּ מַאֲמִירֶךָ וְאַתָּה מַאֲמִירֵנוּ.	We are Your chosen ones and You have chosen us.

Our rabbis tell us that all of our actions matter. Our deeds can help us make the world a better place. Your action can feed the hungry, comfort the sick, and bring a smile to a senior.

The rabbis tell us that all our deeds, good and bad, are noticed and recorded.

בְּרֹאשׁ הַשָּׁנָה יִכָּתֵבוּן,

On Rosh Hashanah [the judgment] is written,

וּבְיוֹם צוֹם כִּפּוּר יֵחָתֵמוּן.

and on the fast of Yom Kippur it is sealed.

But everyone also has a chance to influence the final decison:

וּתְשׁוּבָה וּתְפִלָּה וּצְדָקָה מַעֲבִירִין אֶת־רוֹעַ הַגְּזֵרָה.

Repentance, prayer, and righteousness do away with the severe decree.

It's a Mitzvah 405

יוֹם תְּרוּעָה It shall be a day of shofar blowing
יִהְיֶה לָכֶם for you.

Bamidbar 29:1

It is a mitzvah to listen to the blowing of the שׁוֹפָר. The ba'al tekiyah (shofar blower) sounds a total of 100 notes. The rabbis say that the sounds of the שׁוֹפָר are meant to remind us that רֹאשׁ הַשָּׁנָה is no ordinary holiday. רֹאשׁ הַשָּׁנָה is the day of judgment and the time for us to awaken from our spiritual slumber.

רֹאשׁ הַשָּׁנָה is the time of the year to obtain forgiveness from your teachers, friends, and family for some of the dumb things you have done. It is also the time to promise not to repeat them.

WE ARE AWARE וּנְתַנֶּה תֹּקֶף

The וּנְתַנֶּה תֹּקֶף is the most serious prayer of the day. People are now standing in judgment before Adonai, the judge, waiting for the verdict.

Who will live?

Who will die?

Who by fire?

And who by violence?

The prayer ends on a hopeful note that the verdict is reversible. Prayer, penitence, and righteous deeds can revise the verdict. Now the challenge is in the hands of each of us. We can ignore the warning or choose the path of righteousness.

וּנְתַנֶּה תֹּקֶף קְדֻשַּׁת הַיּוֹם.	We are aware of the holiness of the day.
כִּי הוּא נוֹרָא וְאָיוֹם.	It is awesome and frightening.
וּבוֹ תִנָּשֵׂא מַלְכוּתֶךָ	We praise Your rule
וְיִכּוֹן בְּחֶסֶד כִּסְאֶךָ.	Your throne is based upon mercy.
וְתֵשֵׁב עָלָיו בֶּאֱמֶת.	It is founded on truth.
אֱמֶת כִּי אַתָּה הוּא דַיָּן וּמוֹכִיחַ,	Truly! You are the one who judges,
וְיוֹדֵעַ וָעֵד,	Who proves, knows, and witnesses,
וְכוֹתֵב וְחוֹתֵם,	Who writes and seals,
וְסוֹפֵר וּמוֹנֶה	Who counts
וְתִזְכּוֹר כָּל הַנִּשְׁכָּחוֹת.	And remembers what is forgotten.
וְתִפְתַּח אֶת סֵפֶר הַזִּכְרוֹנוֹת	You open the Book of Remembrances
וּמֵאֵלָיו יִקָּרֵא	And You decide
וְחוֹתָם יַד כָּל אָדָם בּוֹ.	The fate of every human life is in it

On the holy day of יוֹם כִּפּוּר, the tenth day of the month of תִּשְׁרֵי, God determines the future of every human being. On this solemn day, as the Bible commands, Jews do not eat or drink even a sip of water, except for the sick.

At dusk, men, women, and children gather in the בֵּית הַכְּנֶסֶת. The תּוֹרוֹת are taken out of the Holy Ark. The congregation rises. The cantor begins the famous כָּל נִדְרֵי prayer in the chant known round the world. Three times the cantor chants the prayer.

HEBREW WORD BANK

1	יוֹם כִּפּוּר	Day of Atonement
2	כָּל נִדְרֵי	"All the Vows"
3	נְעִילָה	Closing prayer on Yom Kippur
4	יִזְכּוֹר	Memorial prayer
5	יוֹנָה	Jonah
6	תּוֹרָה, תּוֹרוֹת	Torah, Torot
7	שׁוֹפָר	Ram's horn
8	עַל חֵטְא	Yom Kippur prayer of confession
9	תִּשְׁרֵי	Month of Tishrei
10	מַחְזוֹר	High Holiday prayerbooK
11	בֵּית הַכְּנֶסֶת	Synagogue
12	עֲשֶׂרֶת יְמֵי תְּשׁוּבָה	Ten Days of Awe

In the Days of the Inquisition

כָּל means "all," and נִדְרֵי means "vows." The כָּל נִדְרֵי prayer states that all vows and oaths not carried out are canceled.

In the days of the Inquisition in fifteenth-century Spain and Portugal, Jews were often forced to give up their faith. They became Christians outwardly, but secretly continued to observe Jewish customs. These Jews who had to pretend to be Christians are called Marranos.

In the כָּל נִדְרֵי prayer they begged God to release them from vows they had been forced to make when they were pretending to be Christians and to forgive them.

כָּל נִדְרֵי refers only to vows made to God. Promises to other people that we make in the course of everyday life cannot be done away with by reciting a prayer.

This Yom Kippur *Machzor* was a mute witness to the cruel period of the Inquisition in Spain. It was designed in this elongated shape for a special purpose. In case of a surprise visit by officers of the government, Marrano Jews would hide the prayerbook in their wide sleeves, and thus escape detection.

Yom Kippur Day

Services begin early on יוֹם כִּפּוּר day and last until evening. Several times during the day the congregation makes a confession of every possible kind of sin and wrongdoing, just in case any of the sins has been committed unknowingly. This prayer of confession is called עַל חֵטְא. In it we ask forgiveness for such sins as dishonesty, disrespect for parents, cruelty, and the like.

Memorial Prayer

An important part of the יוֹם כִּפּוּר service is the יִזְכּוֹר for the dead. יִזְכּוֹר is recited for the departed on several important holidays–Yom Kippur, Shemini Atzeret, the last day of Passover, and the second day of Shavuot.

יוֹנָה

Reading Jonah

At the יוֹם כִּפּוּר afternoon service the Haftarah is the book of the reading from the prophets יוֹנָה.

In this book, we learn how יוֹנָה fled to the distant city of Nineveh because he wanted to escape the presence of God. But his efforts were in vain, for he learned that God is everywhere. This reading teaches us that no matter where we live, in whatever age or country, God's love embraces all the people on earth.

Ne'ilah

We summon our strength for the last service of the day of יוֹם כִּפּוּר.

It is called נְעִילָה, or "closing." The cantor and the congregation chant:

נְעִילָה

פִּתְחוּ לִי שַׁעֲרֵי צֶדֶק אָבֹא בָם אוֹדֶה יָהּ:

Open for each of us the gates of righteousness;
then shall we enter, praising God.

פְּתַח לָנוּ שַׁעַר. בְּעֵת נְעִילַת שַׁעַר. כִּי פָנָה יוֹם:
הַיּוֹם יִפְנֶה. הַשֶּׁמֶשׁ יָבוֹא וְיִפְנֶה. נָבוֹאָה שְׁעָרֶיךָ:
אָנָּא אֵל נָא. שָׂא נָא. סְלַח־נָא. מְחַל־נָא.
חֲמָל־נָא. רַחֶם־נָא. כַּפֶּר־נָא. כְּבֹשׁ חֵטְא וְעָוֹן:

Open the gate for us now when the gates are closing.
For day is passing, day is passing.
The sun turns home.
Let us come into Your gates.
Please, God, spare . . .
Please forgive . . .
Please have mercy . . .
Please forget.
Please forbear.
And please absolve.
Help us overcome sin and wrong-doing.

בֵּית הַכְּנֶסֶת

At the very end of the evening service, the שׁוֹפָר is blown for the first and only time on יוֹם כִּפּוּר. The note is a long, steady one held as long as the breath of the shofer blower holds out.

יוֹם כִּפּוּר is over. People hurry home to break the fast.

The High Holy Days are at an end.

מַחֲזוֹר

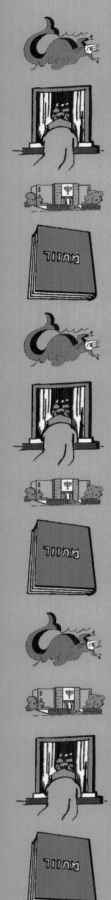

YOM KIPPUR AT HOME

הַדְלָקַת הַנֵּרוֹת לְיוֹם כִּפּוּר

CANDLE LIGHTING FOR YOM KIPPUR

Kiddush is not recited on יוֹם כִּפּוּר, but the traditional
candle lighting blessings are recited.

בָּרוּךְ אַתָּה יְיָ,
אֱלֹהֵינוּ מֶלֶךְ הָעוֹלָם,
אֲשֶׁר קִדְּשָׁנוּ בְּמִצְוֹתָיו,
וְצִוָּנוּ לְהַדְלִיק נֵר
שֶׁל יוֹם הַכִּפּוּרִים.

Praised is Adonai
our God, Ruler of the universe,

who made us holy by the mitzvot,

by commanding us to light candles
for Yom Kippur.

בָּרוּךְ אַתָּה יְיָ,
אֱלֹהֵינוּ מֶלֶךְ הָעוֹלָם,
שֶׁהֶחֱיָנוּ וְקִיְּמָנוּ
וְהִגִּיעָנוּ לַזְּמַן הַזֶּה.

Praised is Adonai,
our God, Ruler of the universe,

who has kept us alive and well

and given us the opportunity to
celebrate this occasion.

It's a Mitzvah 313

אַךְ בֶּעָשׂוֹר לַחֹדֶשׁ הַשְּׁבִיעִי הַזֶּה
יוֹם הַכִּפֻּרִים הוּא
מִקְרָא־קֹדֶשׁ יִהְיֶה לָכֶם
וְעִנִּיתֶם אֶת־נַפְשֹׁתֵיכֶם
וְהִקְרַבְתֶּם אִשֶּׁה לַיהֹוָה.

The tenth day of the seventh month
shall be a Day of Atonement,
a day of holy convocation,
and you shall afflict your souls
and bring an offering to Adonai

(Vayikra 23:27)

The Torah tells us that it is a mitzvah to fast on the tenth day of the month
of תִּשְׁרֵי, which is יוֹם כִּפּוּר.

Our sages tell us to begin the fast just before twilight of the preceding
evening and fast all of the next day, until it is night, twenty-five hours
later.

The ten-day period between רֹאשׁ הַשָּׁנָה and יוֹם כִּפּוּר is called the
עֲשֶׂרֶת יְמֵי תְּשׁוּבָה.

Our sages suggest that during this period we should personally and
sincerely ask our friends, family, and business associates for forgiveness
for any insult and for anything we have wrongfully done to them.

YOM KIPPUR IN THE SYNAGOGUE

כָּל נִדְרֵי ALL PROMISES

כָּל נִדְרֵי is an Aramaic declaration that all promises and vows made by any member of the congregation during the past year shall be null and void if they are not fulfilled.

The cantor and the two or more people who hold the תוֹרוֹת during the chanting recall the ancient court consisting of three people before whom one would appear if seeking to have a promise annulled. כָּל נִדְרֵי is recited three times.

The recitation takes place immediately before יוֹם כִּפּוּר, since the court procedure could not be conducted on a holiday.

כָּל נִדְרֵי held special meaning for Spanish Jews who were compelled to convert during the Spanish Inquisition in 1391–1492. They secretly entered the בֵּית הַכְּנֶסֶת to ask Adonai's forgiveness despite their vows.

No annulment can be made for promises made to another person, a court, or the government.

כָּל נִדְרֵי, — All promises,

וֶאֱסָרֵי, וַחֲרָמֵי, וְקוֹנָמֵי, — pledges, and oaths,

וְכִנּוּיֵי, וְקִנּוּסֵי, וּשְׁבוּעוֹת,

דִּנְדַרְנָא, וּדְאִשְׁתְּבַּעְנָא, וּדְאַחֲרִימְנָא, — which we promise without thinking or meaning to,

וּדְאָסַרְנָא עַל נַפְשָׁתָנָא. — may we be forgiven for them, and good come to us.

מִיּוֹם כִּפֻּרִים זֶה, — From this Yom Kippur

עַד יוֹם כִּפֻּרִים הַבָּא עָלֵינוּ לְטוֹבָה. — until next Yom Kippur.

35

YOM KIPPUR IN THE SYNAGOGUE

אָשַׁמְנוּ WE HAVE SINNED

Jewish tradition holds that we are born with two tendencies: yetzer ha-tov is the tendency to do good, and yetzer ha-ra is the tendency to be contrary. The עֲשֶׂרֶת יְמֵי תְשׁוּבָה offers us an opportunity to turn away from yetzer ha-ra and to do teshuvah and return to the yetzer ha-tov. During the עֲשֶׂרֶת יְמֵי תְשׁוּבָה we recite the Ashamnu prayer, confess our misdeeds, and promise to change.

The יוֹם כִּפּוּר service contains two types of confessionals: the short form and the long form. Both prayers are acrostics, starting from the letter א and ending on the Hebrew letter ת.

SHORT FORM

The Ashamnu is the first part of the confession and deals with twenty-five general types of transgressions, for which people are morally responsible. We lie, we provoke, we rebel, etc. The Ashamnu is the short form and follows the alefbet. Thus it begings :

אָשַׁמְנוּ.	*Aleph*	We have sinned.
בָּגַדְנוּ.	*Bet*	We have acted treacherously.
גָּזַלְנוּ.	*Gimel*	We have stolen.
דִּבַּרְנוּ דֹפִי.	*Dalet*	We have slandered.

LONG FORM

The prayers of confession are:

Note that the two prayers of confession are phrased in the plural. Their purpose is to sensitize us and make us aware of our own actions and the actions of those around us.

The עַל חֵטְא confessional consists of a wide range of sins, far more than any individual could have committed. The reason is it contains not only our individual transgressions, but also those of the Jewish people. Some say that the principle that all Jews are responsible for each other makes all Jews partners. A part of the עַל חֵטְא is :

וְעַל חֵטְא שֶׁחָטָאנוּ לְפָנֶיךָ בְּלָשׁוֹן הָרָע.	For the sin we have committed before You by speaking slander.
עַל חֵטְא שֶׁחָטָאנוּ לְפָנֶיךָ בְּמַשָּׂא וּבְמַתָּן.	For the sin we have committed before You by cheating in business.
עַל חֵטְא שֶׁחָטָאנוּ לְפָנֶיךָ בְּהוֹנָאַת רֵעַ.	And for the sin we have committed before You by hurting other people.

YOM KIPPUR IN THE SYNAGOGUE

נְעִילָה CLOSING

At the time of the ancient Temple, at day's end there was a service called נְעִילָה, meaning "closing". At that time, the gates were closed.

Today we still perform a נְעִילָה service, but now it is the gates of heaven that are closing.

The ark is opened at the start of the נְעִילָה service, because this is the most important service of the day. By keeping the gate of the Ark open, we are saying "Open the gates of heaven for us."

פְּתַח לָנוּ שַׁעַר,	Open the heavenly gates for us,
בְּעֵת נְעִילַת שַׁעַר,	At this moment the gate is closing
כִּי פָנָה יוֹם.	For the day is coming to a close.
הַיּוֹם יִפְנֶה,	This day will fade away,
הַשֶּׁמֶשׁ יָבוֹא וְיִפְנֶה,	The sun will set and slowly fade away.
נָבוֹאָה שְׁעָרֶיךָ.	Let us enter your heavenly gate.
אָנָּא אֵל נָא,	O God, we beg You,
שָׂא נָא,	Forbear,
סְלַח נָא,	Forgive,
מְחַל נָא,	Pardon,
חֲמָל נָא,	Have pity,
רַחֶם־נָא,	Be merciful,
כַּפֶּר־נָא,	Forgive us,
כְּבֹשׁ חֵטְא וְעָוֹן.	Help us conquer our sins.

Before יוֹם כִּפּוּר comes to an end, we recite:

שְׁמַע יִשְׂרָאֵל יְיָ אֱלֹהֵינוּ יְיָ אֶחָד.

Next we recite this phrase three times:

בָּרוּךְ שֵׁם כְּבוֹד מַלְכוּתוֹ לְעוֹלָם וָעֶד.

Next we recite this phrase seven times:

יְיָ הוּא הָאֱלֹהִים.

Now the שׁוֹפָר is blown with a long blast, a tekiah gedolah.
After the שׁוֹפָר is blown, the congregants recite:

לְשָׁנָה הַבָּאָה בִּירוּשָׁלָיִם.

יוֹם כִּפּוּר is over. Time to break the fast.

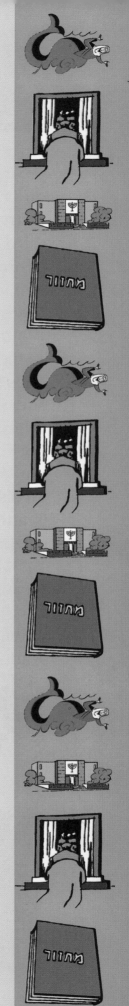

WHY SUKKOT ?

In the history of every people there are great moments that it likes to recall in order to be reminded of the past and to learn a lesson for the future. סוכות is the third of the שָׁלֹשׁ רְגָלִים. The Torah mandates, "Three times each year, every male among you must appear before God." The three times referred to were the holidays of, סוכות, פֶּסַח, and שָׁבֻעוֹת, known in Hebrew as the שָׁלֹשׁ רְגָלִים.

Jews from all parts of Palestine and surrounding countries used to make pilgrimages to the בֵּית הַמִקְדָּשׁ in Jerusalem. Five days after Yom Kippur, the holiest day of the Jewish year, comes סוכות, one of the happiest of all festivals.

Traditionally סוכות is celebrated for nine days. Reform Jews celebrate for eight days and combine the last two days. חַג הַסוכות begins on the fifteenth day of the month of תִּשְׁרֵי. In the Bible, סוכות is known by the names חַג הַסוכות and חַג הָאָסִיף.

After our ancestors left Egypt, the Bible tells us, they wandered for forty years in the desert before they reached the Promised Land.

During that time, they lived in סוכות, booths made of dry palms and branches. The Torah tells us to dwell in booths seven days each year in remembrance of those years of wandering and hardship.

After our ancestors settled in Canaan, they became farmers (Devarim. 16: 14–16) and discovered that the autumn, when סוכות was celebrated, was also the time when they gathered in the crops. So סוכות became a double celebration.

After they left Egypt, the Israelites wandered through the desert for 40 years. They traveled from one oasis to another for cool fresh water and shade from the hot desert sun.

WHY SUKKOT ?

The Pilgrims

Pilgrims were called עוֹלֵי רֶגֶל, meaning "those who go up by foot." They were so called because Jerusalem is located high in the hills of Judea and the pilgrims had to climb by foot to reach the בֵּית הַמִּקְדָּשׁ. Ancient sources state that hundreds of thousands made their way to the בֵּית הַמִּקְדָּשׁ during each of the שָׁלֹשׁ רְגָלִים.

סוּכָּה

Bikkurim

The object of the שָׁלֹשׁ רְגָלִים was to bring בִּכּוּרִים and offer a sacrifice at the בֵּית הַמִּקְדָּשׁ. The Torah also commands, "None shall appear empty-handed. Every person shall give as he is able." (Devarim 16: 16-17).

The Sukkot Pilgrimage

The three שָׁלֹשׁ רְגָלִים festivals, שָׁבְעוֹת, פֶּסַח, and סוּכּוֹת, have both agricultural and historical themes. Sukkot, occurring in the month of תִּשְׁרֵי, has two biblical names: חַג הָאָסִיף and חַג הַסוּכּוֹת. In its חַג הָאָסִיף aspect it is a harvest thanksgiving festival. In its חַג הַסוּכּוֹת aspect it is a historical festival, commemorating God's protection of the Israelites during the forty years in the wilderness after the Exodus from Egypt. The link between the Exodus and the harvest accounts for the timing of חַג הַסוּכּוֹת. According to tradition, the Jews, after leaving Egypt, arrived at the oasis of סוּכּוֹת on the fifteenth of Nisan. It was in סוּכּוֹת that God provided them with סוּכּוֹת (huts) for protection from the sun.

לוּלָב

אֶתְרוֹג

It's a Mitzvah 321

שִׁבְעַת יָמִים	For seven days
תַּקְרִיבוּ אִשֶּׁה לַיהֹוָה;	present offerings;
בַּיּוֹם הַשְּׁמִינִי	on the eighth day
מִקְרָא־קֹדֶשׁ יִהְיֶה לָכֶם,	hold a sacred assembly,
וְהִקְרַבְתֶּם אִשֶּׁה לַיהֹוָה.	and bring an offering to Adonai.
עֲצֶרֶת הוּא,	It is a time of solemn assembly,
כָּל־מְלֶאכֶת עֲבֹדָה לֹא תַעֲשׂוּ.	and do no regular work.

(Vayikra 23:36)

It is a mitzvah not to work on the eighth day of Sukkot, which is the 22nd day of Tishri.

אַרְבָּעָה מִינִים

LET'S CELEBRATE SUKKOT

To show that סוכות was close at hand, it became a custom to erect the סוּכָּה at the end of Yom Kippur. The סוּכָּה is a hut; Its roof is loosely covered with twigs and branches so that the stars can shine through. Everybody helps decorate the סוּכָּה with apples, pomegranates, clusters of grapes, corn, and all kinds of flowers. During סוכות, some people eat all their meals in the סוּכָּה.

The "Four Kinds"

The Torah commands us to take אַרְבָּעָה מִינִים —the אֶתְרוֹג, the לוּלָב, the הֲדַס, and עֲרָבָה of the brook—and rejoice before God for seven days while celebrating the harvest festival.

It was in this way that, our ancestors showed their appreciation for God's goodness. Every morning during the first seven days of סוכות (except on the Sabbath), we take these אַרְבָּעָה מִינִים and recite a blessing. The prayer is recited while one is standing and holding the לוּלָב in the right hand and the אֶתְרוֹג in the left, with the top pointing down. As soon as the blessing is ended, the אֶתְרוֹג is turned over. Then with the אֶתְרוֹג held close to the לוּלָב, so that they are as one unit, they are waved together in six directions. This movement is called נְענוּעִים.

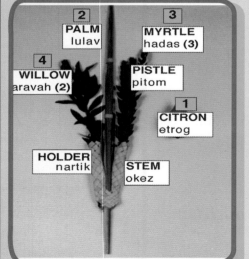

The "four kinds" consist of the citron, palm, myrtle branches, and willows of the brook. Every morning during the Sukkot holiday, we take these "four kinds" and recite a blessing in appreciation for God's goodness.

Hoshanah Rabbah

The name Hoshanah Rabbah means "great help." It is the seventh day of Sukkot.

During the seven days of סוכות, special prayers called הוֹשַׁעְנָא are recited.

In synagogue, there is a special procession around the synagogue. The ark is opened after Musaf, the additional service, and a procession called הַקָּפוֹת takes place. First in line is the cantor, followed by the rabbi, after whom come all the congregants holding an אֶתְרוֹג and לוּלָב. They march around the bimah, or down the aisles, while the cantor chants the הוֹשַׁעְנָא prayer.

Shemini Atzeret

On the eighth day of Sukkot, the אֶתְרוֹג and לוּלָב are laid aside, for this is an entirely new festival, called שְׁמִינִי עֲצֶרֶת, the Eighth Day of Solemn Assembly. Several special features mark the morning service. Memorial prayers, (Yizkor) are said for the dead. A prayer called Geshem ("Rain") is recited. In it, we ask God to provide rain in this season. In the Holy Land, summer is the dry season, when there is no rain at all. It rains only during the winter. And in Israel the crops of the spring depend on the rains of October.

סוּכָּה

לוּלָב

אֶתְרוֹג

אַרְבָּעָה מִינִים

It's a Mitzvah 325

בַּסֻּכֹּת תֵּשְׁבוּ שִׁבְעַת יָמִים. You shall live in booths for seven days.

כָּל־הָאֶזְרָח בְּיִשְׂרָאֵל יֵשְׁבוּ בַּסֻּכֹּת: This means that all native born Israelites shall live in booths.

(Vayikra 23:42)

The Torah tells us that it is a mitzvah to live in a סוּכָּה for seven days from the fifteenth to the twenty-second day of the month of Tishrei.

When we sit in a סוּכָּה and see the stars through the leafy roof, we are reminded of the great miracles that God performed for our ancestors and is still performing for us.

41

SUKKOT AT HOME

הַדְלָקַת הַנֵּרוֹת לְחַג הַסֻּכּוֹת

SUKKOT CANDLE LIGHTING PRAYER

The Torah tells us that on the first day of creation, Adonai started by creating light. We, too, in imitation of Adonai, start the holy festival of סוכות with light.

בָּרוּךְ אַתָּה יְיָ,
Praised is Adonai,

אֱלֹהֵינוּ מֶלֶךְ הָעוֹלָם,
our God, Ruler of the universe,

אֲשֶׁר קִדְּשָׁנוּ בְּמִצְוֹתָיו
who made us holy by the mitzvot

וְצִוָּנוּ לְהַדְלִיק נֵר שֶׁל יוֹם טוֹב.
by commanding us
to light candles for the festival.

בָּרוּךְ אַתָּה יְיָ,
Praised is Adonai,

אֱלֹהֵינוּ מֶלֶךְ הָעוֹלָם,
our God, Ruler of the universe,

שֶׁהֶחֱיָנוּ וְקִיְּמָנוּ
who has kept us alive and well

וְהִגִּיעָנוּ לַזְּמַן הַזֶּה.
and has given us the opportunity
to celebrate this occasion.

? Did You Know?

קֹהֶלֶת

The Book of קֹהֶלֶת is one of the five Megillot, which are in the third section of the Tanach. Its author is traditionally identified as wise King Solomon. קֹהֶלֶת deals with the pursuit of wisdom, pleasure, and wealth. It teaches that wealth and power do not bring happiness.
The Book of קֹהֶלֶת counsels: "Revere God, and observe the commandments."
קֹהֶלֶת is recited in the synagogue on שְׁמִינִי עֲצֶרֶת.

SUKKOT AT HOME

קִדּוּשׁ לְחַג הַסֻּכּוֹת
KIDDUSH FOR SUKKOT

The Kiddush for סֻכּוֹת and שְׁמִינִי עֲצֶרֶת reminds us of our freedom from
Egyptian slavery and the building of the סֻכּוֹת in the desert.
If the holiday begins on Friday, start here.

וַיְהִי־עֶרֶב, וַיְהִי־בְקֶר, יוֹם הַשִּׁשִּׁי.	It was evening and morning on the sixth day.
וַיְכֻלּוּ הַשָּׁמַיִם וְהָאָרֶץ וְכָל־צְבָאָם.	The universe and planet earth and all that was within them had been completed.
וַיְכַל אֱלֹהִים בַּיּוֹם הַשְּׁבִיעִי, מְלַאכְתּוֹ אֲשֶׁר עָשָׂה,	Elohim finished all the work of creation by the seventh day.
וַיִּשְׁבֹּת בַּיּוֹם הַשְּׁבִיעִי	And Elohim rested on the seventh day
מִכָּל מְלַאכְתּוֹ אֲשֶׁר עָשָׂה.	from doing all the work of creation.
וַיְבָרֶךְ אֱלֹהִים אֶת־יוֹם הַשְּׁבִיעִי וַיְקַדֵּשׁ אֹתוֹ,	And Elohim blessed the seventh day and made it holy,
כִּי בוֹ שָׁבַת מִכָּל מְלַאכְתּוֹ	because then Elohim rested from
אֲשֶׁר בָּרָא אֱלֹהִים לַעֲשׂוֹת.	all the work of creation.

If the holiday begins on a weekday, start here.

בָּרוּךְ אַתָּה יְיָ,	Praised is Adonai,
אֱלֹהֵינוּ מֶלֶךְ הָעוֹלָם,	our God, Ruler of the universe,
בּוֹרֵא פְּרִי הַגָּפֶן.	who created the fruit of the vine.
בָּרוּךְ אַתָּה יְיָ,	Praised is Adonai,
אֱלֹהֵינוּ מֶלֶךְ הָעוֹלָם,	our God, Ruler of the universe,
אֲשֶׁר בָּחַר בָּנוּ מִכָּל־עָם,	who chose us from among all people
וְרוֹמְמָנוּ מִכָּל־לָשׁוֹן,	and raised us from among all other languages
וְקִדְּשָׁנוּ בְּמִצְוֹתָיו.	and made us holy with commandments,

continued on page 44

43

SUKKOT AT HOME

וַתִּתֶּן־לָנוּ, יְיָ אֱלֹהֵינוּ, בְּאַהֲבָה,   and in love, gave us

(שַׁבָּתוֹת לִמְנוּחָה),   (Shabbats of rest),

מוֹעֲדִים לְשִׂמְחָה,   festivals of joy,

חַגִּים וּזְמַנִּים לְשָׂשׂוֹן,   and special days of gladness,

אֶת־יוֹם חַג הַסֻּכּוֹת הַזֶּה,   the holiday of Sukkot,

זְמַן שִׂמְחָתֵנוּ,   the time of joy,

הַשְּׁמִינִי חַג הָעֲצֶרֶת הַזֶּה,   the Festival of the Eighth Day,

זְמַן שִׂמְחָתֵנוּ.   the time of joy.

(בְּאַהֲבָה) מִקְרָא קֹדֶשׁ,   God gave us (in love) this holy event, so

זֵכֶר לִיצִיאַת מִצְרָיִם.   that we may remember our Exodus from Egypt.

כִּי בָנוּ בָחַרְתָּ וְאוֹתָנוּ קִדַּשְׁתָּ   You have chosen us and made us holy

מִכָּל הָעַמִּים.   among all the nations.

(וְשַׁבָּת) וּמוֹעֲדֵי קָדְשֶׁךָ, (בְּאַהֲבָה וּבְרָצוֹן)   And gave us Your holy days of joy (and

בְּשִׂמְחָה וּבְשָׂשׂוֹן הִנְחַלְתָּנוּ.   Your Shabbat with love).

בָּרוּךְ אַתָּה יְיָ,   Praised is Adonai,

מְקַדֵּשׁ (הַשַּׁבָּת, וְ)   who makes holy (Shabbat),

יִשְׂרָאֵל וְהַזְּמַנִּים.   Israel, and all the seasons.

בָּרוּךְ אַתָּה יְיָ,   Praised is Adonai,

אֱלֹהֵינוּ מֶלֶךְ הָעוֹלָם,   our God, Ruler of the universe,

שֶׁהֶחֱיָנוּ וְקִיְּמָנוּ   who has kept us alive and well

וְהִגִּיעָנוּ לַזְּמַן הַזֶּה.   and has given us the opportunity to celebrate this occasion.

SUKKOT AT HOME

לֵישֵׁב בַּסֻּכָּה

As we enter the סֻכָּה we recite this special blessing. The סֻכָּה reminds us of the leafy booths in which our ancestors lived as they marched through the desert.

בָּרוּךְ אַתָּה יְיָ,	Praised is Adonai,
אֱלֹהֵינוּ מֶלֶךְ הָעוֹלָם,	our God, Ruler of the universe,
אֲשֶׁר קִדְּשָׁנוּ בְּמִצְוֹתָיו	who made us holy by the mitzvot
וְצִוָּנוּ לֵישֵׁב בַּסֻּכָּה.	and commanded us to stay in the sukkah.

אוּשְׁפִּיזִין

Upon entering the סֻכָּה it is customary to recite a short prayer and symbolically invite our patriarchs and matriarchs as honored, invisible guests (ushpizen). Seven biblical guests and their wives and relatives are invited to join the feast.

אֲזַמִּין לִסְעֻדָּתִי אוּשְׁפִּיזִין עִלָּאִין:	I invite to my meal these heavenly guests:
אַבְרָהָם וְשָׂרָה,	Abraham and Sarah,
יִצְחָק וְרִבְקָה,	Isaac and Rebecca,
יַעֲקֹב רָחֵל וְלֵאָה,	Jacob, Leah, and Rachel,
יוֹסֵף,	Joseph,
מֹשֶׁה, אַהֲרֹן, מִרְיָם,	Moses, Aaron, and Miriam,
וְדָוִד.	and David.

FIRST DAY

בְּמָטוּ מִנְּכוֹן אַבְרָהָם וְשָׂרָה,	May it please you, Abraham and Sarah,
אוּשְׁפִּיזֵי עִלָּאִי,	my heavenly guests,
דְּיַתְבֵי עִמִּי וְעִמָּךְ	that all the other heavenly guests
כָּל אוּשְׁפִּיזֵי עִלָּאִי.	dwell here with me and you.

SECOND DAY

בְּמָטוּ מִנְּכוֹן יִצְחָק וְרִבְקָה,	May it please you, Isaac and Rebecca,
אוּשְׁפִּיזֵי עִלָּאִי,	my heavenly guests,
דְּיַתְבֵי עִמִּי וְעִמָּךְ	that all the heavenly guests
כָּל אוּשְׁפִּיזֵי עִלָּאִי.	dwell here with me and with you.

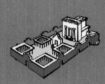

SUKKOT AT HOME

The Torah tells us that the Land of Israel was "a land of milk and honey."
Your ancestors were farmers in the Land of Israel. The אַרְבָּעָה מִינִים are
symbols and part of a ritual which goes back to that agricultural period.
Today Israel grows a large amount of flowers, fruits, and vegetables which
are exported all over the world.

The following two blessings are recited as we wave the לוּלָב and smell the
sweet aroma of the אֶתְרוֹג.

Adonai has numerous names. Sometimes Adonai is called הַמָקוֹם. When
we recite the blessings over the אַרְבָּעָה מִינִים, we wave the לוּלָב up and
down and all around. These נְעַנוּעִים signify that Adonai is everywhere and
in every מָקוֹם.

בָּרוּךְ אַתָּה יְיָ,	Praised is Adonai,
אֱלֹהֵינוּ מֶלֶךְ הָעוֹלָם,	our God, Ruler of the universe, who gave us divine commandments to make us holy
אֲשֶׁר קִדְּשָׁנוּ בְּמִצְוֹתָיו	
וְצִוָּנוּ עַל נְטִילַת לוּלָב.	and commanded us to wave the lulav.
בָּרוּךְ אַתָּה יְיָ,	Praised is Adonai,
אֱלֹהֵינוּ מֶלֶךְ הָעוֹלָם,	our God, Ruler of the universe,
שֶׁהֶחֱיָנוּ וְקִיְּמָנוּ	who has kept us alive and well
וְהִגִּיעָנוּ לַזְּמַן הַזֶּה.	and has given us the opportunity to celebrate this occasion.

Its a Mitzvah 324

וּלְקַחְתֶּם לָכֶם	And you shall take
בַּיוֹם הָרִאשׁוֹן	on the first day
פְּרִי עֵץ הָדָר,	the fruit of a beautiful tree,
כַּפֹּת תְּמָרִים,	the branches of a palm tree,
וַעֲנַף עֵץ עָבֹת,	and boughs of myrtle twigs,
וְעַרְבֵי נָחַל	and willows of the brook.

Vayikra 23:40

It is a mitzvah for you to recite blessings over the אַרְבָּעָה מִינִים:
הֲדַס, עֲרָבָה, אֶתְרוֹג, לוּלָב, and.

Maimonides writes that the proper way to perform this mitzvah is to wave
the לוּלָב in six directions—front, back, left side, right side, upward, and
downward—and to shake the lulav three times in each direction.

These wavings are called נְעַנוּעִים.

SHEMINI ATZERET AT HOME

הַדְלָקַת הַנֵּרוֹת לִשְׁמִינִי הָעֲצֶרֶת
CANDLE LIGHTING FOR SHEMINI ATZERET

בָּרוּךְ אַתָּה יְיָ,

אֱלֹהֵינוּ מֶלֶךְ הָעוֹלָם,

אֲשֶׁר קִדְּשָׁנוּ בְּמִצְוֹתָיו

וְצִוָּנוּ לְהַדְלִיק נֵר שֶׁל יוֹם טוֹב.

Praised is Adonai,
our God, Ruler of the universe,
who made us holy by the mitzvot
by commanding us
to light candles for the festival.

בָּרוּךְ אַתָּה יְיָ,

אֱלֹהֵינוּ מֶלֶךְ הָעוֹלָם,

שֶׁהֶחֱיָנוּ וְקִיְּמָנוּ

וְהִגִּיעָנוּ לַזְּמַן הַזֶּה.

Praised is Adonai,
our God, Ruler of the universe,
who has kept us alive and well
and has given us the opportunity
to celebrate this occasion.

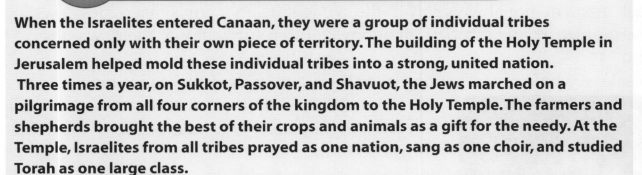

Did You Know?

When the Israelites entered Canaan, they were a group of individual tribes concerned only with their own piece of territory. The building of the Holy Temple in Jerusalem helped mold these individual tribes into a strong, united nation.
Three times a year, on Sukkot, Passover, and Shavuot, the Jews marched on a pilgrimage from all four corners of the kingdom to the Holy Temple. The farmers and shepherds brought the best of their crops and animals as a gift for the needy. At the Temple, Israelites from all tribes prayed as one nation, sang as one choir, and studied Torah as one large class.
Today, wherever there are a number of Jews, there is a miniature temple called the synagogue. On Shabbat, on Jewish holidays, and on special occasions, entire families pilgrimage to the synagogue to pray and sing and study as one large, united people.
Raise your voice! Sing, pray, and study Torah with your fellow worshippers.
Exalt, be happy, raise your voice, and join your prayer with those of your fellow Jews.

בְּשִׂמְחָה וּבְשָׂשׂוֹן הִנְחַלְתָּנוּ.

With joy and happiness You gave us a heritage.

47

LET'S CELEBRATE SIMCHAT TORAH

Each week in the synagogue we read another portion of the תּוֹרָה, going from the first chapter of Bereshit to the last chapter of Devarim. On שִׂמְחַת־תּוֹרָה, the day right after שְׁמִינִי עֲצֶרֶת, the twenty-third day of Tishrei, Jews all over the world read the very last portion of the Torah's fifth book, Devarim, and then begin reading the תּוֹרָה all over again from the beginning.

HEBREW WORD BANK

1 שִׂמְחַת־תּוֹרָה	Rejoicing with the Torah
2 שְׁמִינִי עֲצֶרֶת	Eighth day of Sukkot
3 הַקָּפוֹת	Proccesions with the Torah
4 כָּל הַנְּעָרִים	All the children
5 חֲתַן תּוֹרָה	Groom of the Torah
6 חֲתַן בְּרֵאשִׁית	Groom of Bereshit
7 אַתָּה הָרְאֵתָ לָדַעַת	You have learned
8 תּוֹרָה, תּוֹרוֹת	Torah, torot
9 דֶּגֶל, דְּגָלִים	Flag, flags

Simchat Torah Observances

The שִׂמְחַת־תּוֹרָה holiday is a festive, joy-filled time which marks this happy occasion. The תּוֹרוֹת robed in their brilliantly colored, velvet mantels are taken carefully out of the Ark and held lovingly aloft. Everyone dances around them, waving דְּגָלִים and singing loudly. The whole congregation circles the synagogue in processions called הַקָּפוֹת.

How Simchat Torah Is Celebrated in Israel

In Israel הַקָּפוֹת do not always stay in the synagogue. In many synagogues, Jews dance around, carrying תּוֹרוֹת, with happy children surrounding them, waving bright דְּגָלִים.

In Jerusalem, whole congregations leave their synagogues and dance their way to the Kotel, the Western Wall, with תּוֹרוֹת in their arms. The holiday's name, שִׂמְחַת־תּוֹרָה, perfectly expresses the mood of the moment.

It means "Rejoicing with the Torah."

The Hakafot

The הַקָּפוֹת are introduced by the reading of a collection of biblical verses called אַתָּה הָרְאֵתָ לָדַעַת. Each word is read by the cantor or a member of the congregation, then it is repeated by the participants. All the members of the congregation are given the opportunity to carry a תּוֹרָה during the הַקָּפוֹת.

A ba'al koreh reads the Torah.

48

Consecration

In many Reform temples and Conservative synagogues a beautiful ceremony called Consecration is held. The children who will be starting religious school that year are called to the bimah and each is presented with a miniature תּוֹרָה.

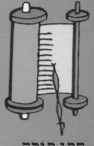

חֲתַן תּוֹרָה

The Morning Service

At the morning service on שִׂמְחַת-תּוֹרָה everyone over thirteen years of age is called to the תּוֹרָה to recite the blessing over the reading of the last sidrah, or portion, of the Book of Devarim. The last person to be called up is the חֲתַן תּוֹרָה (bridegroom of the Torah), because he has the great honor of reciting the blessing over the conclusion of the Five Books of Moses. Then another person is called for the reading of the first chapter in Genesis; he is called the חֲתַן בְּרֵאשִׁית. Individuals who are called to participate in the Torah reading are said to have an aliyah.

חֲתַן בְּרֵאשִׁית

Kol Ha-Ne'arim

Just before these two are called, all the children under the age of thirteen come up to the תּוֹרָה. A large tallit is spread like a canopy over their heads. All together, in one voice, they recite the blessing over the Torah. This is called כָּל הַנְּעָרִים and it marks the one time during the Jewish year when even the smallest girls and boys are given the honor of being called to the תּוֹרָה. In happiness and festivity, שִׂמְחַת-תּוֹרָה slowly draws to a close, ending the High Holy Day season.

הַקָּפוֹת

תּוֹרָה

דֶּגֶל

49

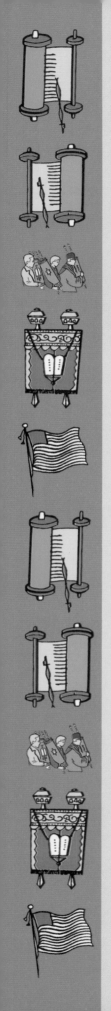

אַתָּה הָרְאֵתָ לָדַעַת

YOU HAVE BEEN TAUGHT TO KNOW

The הַקָּפוֹת are introduced with the prayer אַתָּה הָרְאֵתָ לָדַעַת, a collection of biblical verses in praise of God and Torah.
In some synagogues the cantor reads a verse and then the congregation repeats it. In other synagogues each verse is read by a different member of the congregation. You can also participate in the mitzvah and read a verse. Open up your Siddur and find the אַתָּה הָרְאֵתָ לָדַעַת prayer and start practicing.

אַתָּה הָרְאֵתָ לָדַעַת	You have been taught to know
כִּי יְהֹוָה הוּא הָאֱלֹהִים.	That Adonai is God.
אֵין עוֹד מִלְבַדּוֹ.	There is none other than Him.
לְעֹשֵׂה נִפְלָאוֹת גְּדֹלוֹת לְבַדּוֹ	He alone does wondrous deeds,
כִּי לְעוֹלָם חַסְדּוֹ.	for His lovingkindness is eternal.
אֵין כָּמוֹךָ בָאֱלֹהִים, אֲדֹנָי,	There is none like You among the divine, Adonai,
וְאֵין כְּמַעֲשֶׂיךָ.	And there are no deeds such as Yours.
יְהִי כְבוֹד יְהֹוָה לְעוֹלָם.	May Adonai's glory be eternal.
יִשְׂמַח יְהֹוָה בְּמַעֲשָׂיו.	May Adonai rejoice in His deeds.
יְהִי שֵׁם יְהֹוָה מְבֹרָךְ	May Adonai's name be praised
מֵעַתָּה וְעַד עוֹלָם.	now and forever.
יְהִי יְהֹוָה אֱלֹהֵינוּ עִמָּנוּ	May Adonai our God be with us
כַּאֲשֶׁר הָיָה עִם אֲבוֹתֵינוּ.	As He was with our ancestors.
אַל יַעַזְבֵנוּ וְאַל יִטְּשֵׁנוּ.	May He not leave us nor forsake us.
וְאִמְרוּ: "הוֹשִׁיעֵנוּ, אֱלֹהֵי יִשְׁעֵנוּ."	Say: "Save us, Adonai, our redeemer."

הוֹשִׁיעָה נָּא

The הוֹשִׁיעָה נָּא prayers are recited while the congregation marches around the synagogue seven times. When asking God to save us, we remind God of how He saved our ancestors in the past. In so doing, we hope that God will be as merciful with us as with our ancestors.

Throughout the seven הַקָּפוֹת numerous prayers recited, and two words appear over and over: הוֹשִׁיעָה נָּא.

אָנָּא יְיָ,	Please God,
הוֹשִׁיעָה נָּא;	save us;
אָנָּא יְיָ,	Please God,
הַצְלִיחָה נָא;	prosper us;
אָנָּא יְיָ,	Please God,
עֲנֵנוּ בְיוֹם קָרְאֵנוּ.	answer us when we call;

לֵב יִשְׂרָאֵל THE HEART OF ISRAEL

On שִׂמְחַת־תּוֹרָה we read the last section of the תּוֹרָה and then the first section starting a new תּוֹרָה cycle. The last letter of the תּוֹרָה is the letter ל in the word יִשְׂרָאֵל. The first letter in the תּוֹרָה is the letter ב in the word בְּרֵאשִׁית. Put these two letters together and they spell לֵב, which means heart. The תּוֹרָה is the path of the לֵב. It is the תּוֹרָה that has kept the hearts of the Jewish people alive and well.

This is how the Torah begins:

בְּרֵאשִׁית בָּרָא אֱלֹהִים	When Elohim began to create
אֵת הַשָּׁמַיִם וְאֵת הָאָרֶץ,	heaven and earth,
וְהָאָרֶץ הָיְתָה תֹהוּ וָבֹהוּ.	—the earth being formless and void.
וְחֹשֶׁךְ עַל־פְּנֵי תְהוֹם	Darkness was on the face of the deep
וְרוּחַ אֱלֹהִים מְרַחֶפֶת	and the spirit of Elohim hovered
עַל־פְּנֵי הַמָּיִם.	over the waters.
וַיֹּאמֶר אֱלֹהִים "יְהִי אוֹר!"	Elohim said, "Let there be light!"
וַיְהִי־אוֹר.	And there was light.
וַיַּרְא אֱלֹהִים אֶת־הָאוֹר כִּי־טוֹב.	Elohim saw that the light was good.

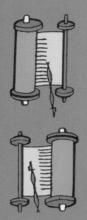

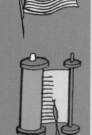

TORAH BLESSINGS בִּרְכוֹת הַתּוֹרָה

שִׂמְחַת־תּוֹרָה is happy time. Let's celebrate! We sing, parade, and honor the תּוֹרָה by reciting blessings. People who are honored are given *aliyot* and are called up to the תּוֹרָה and recite blessings.

Before and after the תּוֹרָה reading they recite "thank you" blessings.

This is the "thank you" blessing before the reading of the תּוֹרָה selection:

בָּרְכוּ אֶת־יְיָ הַמְּבֹרָךְ.	Praised is Adonai who is to be praised.
בָּרוּךְ יְיָ הַמְּבֹרָךְ לְעוֹלָם וָעֶד.	Praised is Adonai who is to be praised forever and ever.

בָּרוּךְ אַתָּה יְיָ,	Praised is Adonai,
אֱלֹהֵינוּ מֶלֶךְ הָעוֹלָם,	our God, Ruler of the universe,
אֲשֶׁר בָּחַר־בָּנוּ מִכָּל־הָעַמִּים	who chose us from all others
וְנָתַן לָנוּ אֶת־תּוֹרָתוֹ.	and gave us His Torah
בָּרוּךְ אַתָּה יְיָ, נוֹתֵן הַתּוֹרָה.	Praised is Adonai, giver of the Torah.

This is the "thank you" blessing after the תּוֹרָה reading selection:

בָּרוּךְ אַתָּה יְיָ,	Praised is Adonai,
אֱלֹהֵינוּ מֶלֶךְ הָעוֹלָם,	our God, Ruler of the universe,
אֲשֶׁר נָתַן־לָנוּ תּוֹרַת אֱמֶת,	who gave us the Torah of truth,
וְחַיֵּי עוֹלָם נָטַע בְּתוֹכֵנוּ.	and planted eternal life within us.
בָּרוּךְ אַתָּה יְיָ,	Praised is Adonai,
נוֹתֵן הַתּוֹרָה.	giver of the Torah.

SIMCHAT TORAH IN SONG

כִּי מִצִּיּוֹן תֵּצֵא תוֹרָה
FROM ZION THE TORAH WILL GO FORTH

This prayer is recited during the תוֹרָה reading
ceremony on שִׂמְחַת־תּוֹרָה.

כִּי מִצִּיּוֹן תֵּצֵא תוֹרָה,

וּדְבַר יְיָ מִירוּשָׁלָיִם.

From Zion the Torah will go forth,
and the word of Adonai
from Jerusalem.

בָּרוּךְ שֶׁנָּתַן תּוֹרָה

לְעַמּוֹ יִשְׂרָאֵל בִּקְדֻשָּׁתוֹ.

Praised be the One who gave the
Torah
in all its holiness to the
people of Israel.

שִׂישׂוּ וְשִׂמְחוּ BE HAPPY

שִׂמְחַת־תּוֹרָה is a time for rejoicing. This happy song
is sung during the הַקָּפוֹת procession.

שִׂישׂוּ וְשִׂמְחוּ
בְּשִׂמְחַת תּוֹרָה,
וּתְנוּ כָבוֹד לַתּוֹרָה.

Be happy!
It's Simchat Torah.
Honor the Torah.

נָגִיל וְנָשִׂישׂ בְּזֹאת הַתּוֹרָה
כִּי הִיא לָנוּ עֹז וְאוֹרָה.

Rejoice with this Torah
Because it is our strength and our light.

תּוֹרָה הִיא עֵץ חַיִּים
לְכֻלָּם חַיִּים,
כִּי עַמְּךְ מְקוֹר חַיִּים.

The Torah is a tree of life
for all living creatures,
because it is a source of life.

אַשְׁרֵיכֶם יִשְׂרָאֵל,
אֲשֶׁר בָּחַר בָּכֶם אֵל
וְהִנְחִילְכֶם הַתּוֹרָה.

Be happy, Israel,
that you are the fortunate nation
that has the Torah.

WHY CHANUKAH?

When the Persians ruled over Palestine, from 536 to 336 B.C.E., the Jews were left in peace. Although a Persian official governed יְרוּשָׁלַיִם, he did not interfere with the Jewish community and the authority of the rabbis.

But Alexader the Great, a young and brilliant Greek general, changed everything when he conquered the Persian Empire in 336 B.C.E. Since the Persian Empire included Palestine, the Jews now had יְוָנִים as rulers instead of Persians. After Alexander's death, his empire was split up among his generals, and Palestine fell into the hands of the יְוָנִים. The new יְוָנִים rulers tried to force all their people to follow Greek customs and worship idols.

But many Jews, who loved their ancient heritage, refused to worship the Syrian idols. These traditional Jews began to think of resisting the יְוָנִים, who sought to take away their religious freedom.

HEBREW WORD BANK

חֲנוּכָּה	1	Feast of Lights
מוֹדִיעִין	2	Town of Modein
יְרוּשָׁלַיִם	3	Jerusalem
בֵּית-הַמִּקְדָּשׁ	4	Holy Temple
יְוָנִים	5	Greeks
יְהוּדָה הַמַּכַּבִּי	6	Judah Maccabee
מַתִּתְיָהוּ	7	Mattathias
כִּסְלֵו	8	The month of the Kislev
מְנוֹרָה	9	Menorah

The Resistance

One day the resistance against the יְוָנִים came to a head. It happened in מוֹדִיעִין , the hometown of מַתִּתְיָהוּ, a member of a priestly family, the Hasmoneans, and the father of five strong sons. מַתִּתְיָהוּ was commanded to bow down and worship the Greek idol. But the proud Jewish leader מַתִּתְיָהוּ refused to violate his Jewish ideals and values. Instead of bowing down to the idol, he called upon the Jews to attack the יְוָנִים and then follow him to the hills. Many Jews joined the revolt.

When מַתִּתְיָהוּ died his son יְהוּדָה הַמַּכַּבִּי, who was so strong that he was called Maccabee ("the hammer"), took the leadership. Soon יְהוּדָה הַמַּכַּבִּי and his courageous warriors drove the יְוָנִים out of Israel.

In 164 B.C.E., יְהוּדָה הַמַּכַּבִּי and his freedom fighters defeated the army of the יְוָנִים and were able to reclaim their beloved and holy capital city, יְרוּשָׁלַיִם. They had won the right to worship in their own way and to lives their life as Jews once again.

54

WHY CHANUKAH?

The Miracle of the Oil

When the victorious Jews reached the בֵּית־הַמִּקְדָּשׁ, they were sadly disappointed at its condition. It was filthy, neglected, and filled with statues of יְוָנִים gods. The בֵּית־הַמִּקְדָּשׁ had to be purified. The מְנוֹרָה had to be relit, but there was only one small flask of pure holy oil to be found. This was just enough to keep the light burning for only one night. By a miracle, the oil in the מְנוֹרָה burned for eight days.

מְנוֹרָה

The Holiday of Chanukah

Full of hope and joy, the Jews rebuilt their altar, cleansed the filth left by the יְוָנִים, and made new holy vessels. On the twenty-fifth of כִּסְלֵו, they were ready to rededicate the Temple. On that day, יְהוּדָה הַמַּכַּבִּי announced a holiday for the dedication of the בֵּית־הַמִּקְדָּשׁ—eight days for the miraculous burning of the holy oil. Today Jews everywhere keep alive the memory of the proud, courageous Maccabees and their triumph by lighting חֲנוּכָּה candles. Each night of חֲנוּכָּה, we light one more candle until, on the final night of חֲנוּכָּה, all eight candles burn brightly.

מַתִּתְיָהוּ

יְהוּדָה הַמַּכַּבִּי

  ## Did You Know?

Today we know more about the חֲנוּכָּה because of the books of Maccabees. First and Second Maccabees belong to a group of post-biblical writings known as the Apocrypha. The original version of this book, written in Hebrew, was lost. Fortunately, the Hebrew text had been translated into Greek. It was preserved in the Septuagint, the Greek version of the Bible. Although the authors of Maccabees are unknown, several facts about them are known. They were Jews who lived sometime after the Maccabean revolt. From their firsthand knowledge, it is believed that they were familiar with the events of the uprising. The text starts with a summary history of the conquest of Alexander the Great and the origin of the Seleucid Empire. It retells historical events from Antiochus IV (175 B.C.E.) to the death of Simon the Hasmonean in 135 B.C.E.

יְוָנִים

LET'S CELEBRATE CHANUKAH

חֲנוּכָּה is a happy festival. It is marked by the lighting of נֵרוֹת in the home, beginning with one נֵר on the first night and adding one additional one on each successive night of the holiday.

נֵרוֹת come forty-four to the box—enough for all eight nights of חֲנוּכָּה. Each night we first light one נֵר that acts as the שַׁמָּשׁ (which means "one who serves") and with that נֵר we light the other נֵרוֹת.

The oldest historical sources that deal with the festival of חֲנוּכָּה are ancient works known as the Books of the Maccabees. They tell us how יְהוּדָה הַמַּכַּבִּי and his brothers defeated the Syrians and recaptured the בֵּית־הַמִּקְדָשׁ.

They cleansed it and then rededicated it on the twenty-fifth day of the month of כִּסְלֵו. Slowly, the custom of lighting חֲנוּכָּה lights in every Jewish home was developed until חֲנוּכָּה became the widespread festival that it is today.

HEBREW WORD BANK

מָעוֹז צוּר	1	Chanukah song
נֵר, נֵרוֹת	2	Candles, candles
סְבִיבוֹן	3	Spinning top
לְבִיבוֹת	4	Potato pancakes
שַׁמָּשׁ	5	Helper candle
חֲנוּכִיָּה	6	Chanukah menorah
נ,ג,ה,שׁ	7	Four Hebrew Draydel letters
דְמֵי חֲנוּכָּה	8	Chanukah gelt (money)

For All to See

So that everyone may know that חֲנוּכָּה is here, we place the נֵרוֹת near a window facing the street. The lighting ceremony is accompanied by blessings and followed by song. The most popular חֲנוּכָּה song is מָעוֹז צוּר, or "Rock of Ages".

There are no special חֲנוּכָּה services in the synagogue. At the regular evening service, however, the נֵרוֹת are lit just as they are at home. Services during חֲנוּכָּה also contain a number of additional prayers. One is Hallel, which consists of selections from the Book of Psalms. Another is Al Ha-Nissim ("For the Miracles").

A family Chanukah celebration

חֲנוּכִּיָה

Chanukah Foods

A favorite חֲנוּכָּה food is latkes, or לְבִיבוֹת. Some say that we eat לְבִיבוֹת because they are fried in oil. The oil reminds us of the miraculous tiny jar of oil which burned for eight days.

The Draydel

You can expect דְמֵי חֲנוּכָּה on this holiday, and you may try to increase your share by playing a game of סְבִיבוֹן. For this game you need a סְבִיבוֹן, or four-sided top, whose four Hebrew letters נ,ג,ה,שׁ stand for נֵס גָּדוֹל הָיָה שָׁם—"a great miracle happened there."

Since the Middle Ages, the popular little סְבִיבוֹן has been part of Chanukah fun everywhere. In Eastern Europe the tops were made of lead.

Spin it, and it tells you: Nun נ, you take nothing from the pot; Gimel ג, you take all; Hay ה, you get half; Shin שׁ, you put something in.

דְמֵי חֲנֻכָּה

The Chanukah Menorah–Chanukiah

When יְהוּדָה הַמַכַּבִּי triumphantly conquered יְרוּשָׁלַיִם, the lamps of the Temple מְנוֹרָה were relit and the rededication of the בֵּית־הַמִקְדָשׁ was celebrated for eight days with feasting and song.

The חֲנוּכִּיָה became recognized as a symbol of our people's love for liberty. It shone in the synagogue, it glowed in the home, it guided Jews throughout their lives and often even accompanied them when they died, as an emblem on their tombstones.

When our ancestors made the first חֲנוּכִּיָה, they knew that it was forbidden to imitate the seven-branched candelabrum of the בֵּית־הַמִקְדָשׁ. Besides, they wished to commemorate the little jar of oil that had lasted for eight days when the בֵּית־הַמִקְדָשׁ was rededicated. For that reason, a special חֲנוּכָּה lamp was designed for the Festival of Light, with an individual shaft for the שַׁמָשׁ (servant) which is used to light the other candles.

This special menorah is called חֲנוּכִּיָה. In every generation the חֲנוּכִּיָה reminds us of our heroic past and rekindles hope and faith in the future.

נֵרוֹת

סְבִיבוֹן

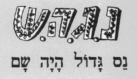

נֵס גָּדוֹל הָיָה שָׁם

CHANUKAH AT HOME

הַדְלָקַת הַנֵרוֹת לַחֲנֻכָּה
CANDLE LIGHTING BLESSINGS

The holiday of חֲנוּכָּה is eight days long, and we light the חֲנוּכִּיָה for each of the eight days. Candle lit starts on the first night with one single נֵר, and on each following night we add one more נֵר until all eight נֵרוֹת are lit. Each night the נֵרוֹת are lit by the שַׁמָשׁ.
On the first night of חֲנֻכָּה we recite the following three blessings.
On all other nights we recite only the first two blessings.

בָּרוּךְ אַתָּה יְיָ,   Praised is Adonai,

אֱלֹהֵינוּ מֶלֶךְ הָעוֹלָם,   our God, Ruler of the universe

אֲשֶׁר קִדְּשָׁנוּ בְּמִצְוֹתָיו   who made us holy by the mitzvot,

וְצִוָּנוּ לְהַדְלִיק נֵר שֶׁל חֲנֻכָּה.   and commanded us to light Chanukah candles.

בָּרוּךְ אַתָּה יְיָ,   Praised is Adonai,

אֱלֹהֵינוּ מֶלֶךְ הָעוֹלָם,   our God, Ruler of the universe,

שֶׁעָשָׂה נִסִּים לַאֲבוֹתֵינוּ   who performed miracles for our ancestors

בַּיָּמִים הָהֵם בַּזְּמַן הַזֶּה.   in those days, at this season.

בָּרוּךְ אַתָּה יְיָ,   Praised is Adonai

אֱלֹהֵינוּ מֶלֶךְ הָעוֹלָם,   our God, Ruler of the universe,

שֶׁהֶחֱיָנוּ, וְקִיְּמָנוּ   who has kept us alive and well

וְהִגִּיעָנוּ לַזְּמַן הַזֶּה.   and has given us the opportunity to celebrate this occasion.

58

הַנֵּרוֹת הַלָּלוּ

After lighting the Chanukiah you recite:

הַנֵּרוֹת הַלָּלוּ אָנוּ מַדְלִיקִים	These lights, which we kindle
עַל הַנִּסִּים, וְעַל הַנִּפְלָאוֹת,	For the miracles, for the salvations,
וְעַל הַתְּשׁוּעוֹת, וְעַל הַמִּלְחָמוֹת,	For the help, for the battles,
שֶׁעָשִׂיתָ לַאֲבוֹתֵינוּ	Which You fought for our ancestors
בַּיָּמִים הָהֵם	In those long ago times
בַּזְּמַן הַזֶּה,	At this time of year
עַל יְדֵי כֹּהֲנֶיךָ הַקְּדוֹשִׁים.	With the help of Your holy priests.

וְכָל שְׁמוֹנַת יְמֵי חֲנֻכָּה,	During these eight days of Chanukah
הַנֵּרוֹת הַלָּלוּ קֹדֶשׁ הֵם,	The lights are holy
וְאֵין לָנוּ רְשׁוּת לְהִשְׁתַּמֵּשׁ בָּהֶם.	And we are not permitted to use them ordinarily.
אֶלָּא לִרְאוֹתָם בִּלְבָד	We gaze at them
כְּדֵי לְהוֹדוֹת	And express thanks and praise
וּלְהַלֵּל לְשִׁמְךָ הַגָּדוֹל,	To Your great Name,
עַל נִסֶּיךָ,	For Your miracles,
וְעַל נִפְלְאוֹתֶיךָ,	Your wonders,
וְעַל יְשׁוּעוֹתֶיךָ:	And Your protection.

It's a Mitzvah D'rabanan

LIGHTING CHANUKAH CANDLES

חֲנוּכָּה candles are lit at home on all eight nights of חֲנוּכָּה. Many temples and religious schools also have public candle-lighting ceremonies for the whole community. On the first night one נֵר is lit, on the second night two נֵרוֹת, and so on. The נֵרוֹת are placed in a special menorah, or candelabrum, called a חֲנוּכִּיָה. The חֲנוּכִּיָה has holders for nine נֵרוֹת, one for each day and a ninth called a שַׁמָּשׁ.

The word שַׁמָּשׁ means "servant." The שַׁמָּשׁ, or servant candle, is lit first. Then it is used to light the other נֵרוֹת.

CHANUKAH AT HOME

מָעוֹז צוּר
ROCK OF AGES

After the נֵרוֹת are lit it is customary to sing the hymn "Maoz Tzur". This hymn was composed in the thirteenth century by an unknown poet called Mordechai.

מָעוֹז צוּר יְשׁוּעָתִי	Rock of ages, my salvation
לְךָ נָאֶה לְשַׁבֵּחַ.	To praise You is a delight.
תִּכּוֹן בֵּית תְּפִלָּתִי.	Restore my Temple of Prayer.
וְשָׁם תּוֹדָה נְזַבֵּחַ,	There we will bring an offering of thanks,
לְעֵת תָּכִין מַטְבֵּחַ	For You have prepared the defeat
מִצָּר הַמְנַבֵּחַ.	Of the godless foe.
אָז אֶגְמוֹר, בְּשִׁיר מִזְמוֹר	Now I will sing a hymn of praise,
חֲנֻכַּת הַמִּזְבֵּחַ.	After the dedication of the altar.

? Did You Know?

How was the original Temple menorah constructed?
The Torah (Shemot 25: 31-40) provides the construction details of the Temple menorah. It was made by Bezalel and hammered out of a solid slab of gold. According to the Torah, it stood seven feet tall, weighed 100 pounds, and was seven-branched.

According to some commentators, the seven-branched מְנוֹרָה represents the creation of the world in six days and the center light is for the seventh day—the Sabbath.

Our sages say that the original Mosaic menorah was concealed by the priests prior to the destruction of the First Temple and has never been found.
The מְנוֹרָה of the Second Temple was made to resemble the one in the Tabernacle, as shown on the relief on the Arch of Titus. It shows the מְנוֹרָה carried on poles on the shoulders of Roman soldiers in a triumphal procession through the streets of Rome.

CHANUKAH IN SONG

מִי יְמַלֵּל גְּבוּרוֹת יִשְׂרָאֵל

מִי יְמַלֵּל	Who can retell
גְּבוּרוֹת יִשְׂרָאֵל?	the miracles that happened to us?
אוֹתָן מִי יִמְנֶה?	Who can count them?
הֵן בְּכָל דּוֹר	In every age
יָקוּם הַגִּבּוֹר גּוֹאֵל הָעָם.	A hero or sage came to our aid.
שְׁמַע!	Listen!
בַּיָּמִים הָהֵם בַּזְּמַן הַזֶּה,	In days of old in Israel's ancient land,
מַכַּבִּי מוֹשִׁיעַ וּפוֹדֶה.	Judah Maccabee led his faithful band.
וּבְיָמֵינוּ כָּל עַם יִשְׂרָאֵל,	And now all Israel must as one arise,
יִתְאַחֵד, יָקוּם וְיִגָּאֵל.	Redeem itself through deed and sacrifice.

סְבִיבוֹן סֹב, סֹב, סֹב!

סְבִיבוֹן סֹב, סֹב, סֹב!	Dreidel, spin, spin, spin!
חֲנֻכָּה הוּא חַג טוֹב.	Chanukah is a good holiday.
חֲנֻכָּה הוּא חַג טוֹב.	Chanukah is a good holiday.
סְבִיבוֹן סֹב, סֹב, סֹב!	Dreidel, spin, spin, spin!
חַג שִׂמְחָה הוּא לָעָם.	It is a holiday of joy for all the nation.
נֵס גָּדוֹל הָיָה שָׁם.	A great miracle happened there.
נֵס גָּדוֹל הָיָה שָׁם	A great miracle happened there
חַג שִׂמְחָה הוּא לָעָם.	For the whole nation.

WHY TU B'SHEVAT ?

The Bible commands the Jewish people not to destroy עֵצִים even when battling in a city. "You may eat of them, but you must not cut them down." The rabbis said that when one chops down a fruit-bearing עֵץ, the cry of the עֵץ goes from one עֵץ of the world to the others.

Flowers and עֵצִים and all growing things mean so much to every human being. Our ancestors knew this.

They realized that עֵצִים are among our best friends. עֵצִים help feed and clothe us. They give us wood for our houses, paper for books, fruit to eat, and shade from the hot sun. עֵצִים keep the soil rich and fertile, and they give beauty to the world.

Tu Equals Fifteen

Our ancestors were aware of the importance of עֵצִים, and they set aside the fifteenth day of the month of שְׁבָט (Chamishah Asar B'Shevat) as Jewish Arbor Day.

It is usually called ט"וּ בִּשְׁבָט, because the abbrevation ט"וּ represents the two Hebrew letters that numerically equal חֲמִשָׁה עָשָׂר. In Israel, the rainy season lasts until February. Then the first buds on the עֵצִים appear, and lo, it's ט"וּ בִּשְׁבָט ! It was in the Mishnah that רֹאשׁ הַשָׁנָה לָאִילָנוֹת received its name. Long before that, the Torah showed the way. The Torah says בַּל תַּשְׁחִית . Fruit עֵצִים must not be cut down even in time of war (Devarim. 20).

The Torah itself is called a "tree of life." King David in the book of Psalms, says that a righteous person i "like an עֵץ planted by the streams of water."

	Hebrew	English
1	ט"וּ בִּשְׁבָט	Fifteenth of Shevat
2	רֹאשׁ הַשָׁנָה לָאִילָנוֹת	New Year of the Trees
3	שְׁבָט	Month of Shevat
4	ט"וּ	Fifteen
5	חַג הַפֵּרוֹת	Holiday of Fruits
6	חֲמִשָׁה עָשָׂר	Fifteen
7	מָעוֹת פֵּרוֹת	Tu B'shevat food fund
8	בַּל תַּשְׁחִית	Do not destroy
9	חֲמִשָׁה עָשָׂר	Fifteen
10	עֵץ, עֵצִים	Tree, trees

HAMISHAH ASAR BISHVAT
חֲמִשָׁה עָשָׂר בִּשְׁבָט

62

WHY TU B'SHEVAT ?

ט"וּ בִּשְׁבָט has two other names which describe its origin: חַג הַפֵּרוֹת (the Holiday of Fruits) and רֹאשׁ הַשָּׁנָה לָאִילָנוֹת the New Year of the Trees. There are many references to עֵצִים in the Bible, showing our love for עֵצִים and telling how they were used in important ways.

Ancient Tu B'Shevat Customs

Many customs grew around ט"וּ בִּשְׁבָט. In ancient Palestine, it was customary to plant an עֵץ when a child was born: a cedar for a boy, and a cypress for a girl. The cedar stood for height and strength, the cypress for tenderness and fragrance. When the children grew up and were married, branches from their trees were cut and used to support the bridal canopy, for good luck. Between birth and marriage they cared for their own עֵצִים. Through this custom everyone learned to love עֵצִים.

In sixteenth–century Palestine, the people of some Jewish communities drank four cups of wine on ט"וּ בִּשְׁבָט. The first cup was white wine to symbolize winter. The second was rosé, for spring. The third: deep red, for summer. The fourth: red mixed with white to symbolize fall.

Another unusual custom was observed in the town of Safed in Israel long ago. On ט"וּ בִּשְׁבָט the inhabitants would do their best to sample at least fifteen (for חֲמִשָּׁה עָשָׂר, which equals 15) different kinds of fruit! Finally, a touching custom was followed by Sephardic Jews in the sixteenth century. They had a מְעוֹת פֵּרוֹת fund: money was collected to provide fruit for the poor on ט"וּ בִּשְׁבָט.

יִשְׂרָאֵל

פֵּרוֹת

ט"וּ

עֵץ, עֵצִים

LET'S CELEBRATE TU B'SHEVAT

In modern Israel, ט״וּ בִּשְׁבָט marks the end of the rainy season and is celebrated in all its ancient glory. In 1949, on the first ט״וּ בִּשְׁבָט after the Jewish state gained its independence, thousands of people gathered to plant life-giving עֵצִים in a forest which will one day contain six million עֵצִים –the number of Jews killed in the Holocaust by Hitler's wrath. It is known as the Forest of the Martyrs. ט״וּ בִּשְׁבָט also reminds us of the way יִשְׂרָאֵל has bloomed under the tender care of the חֲלוּצִים.

Jewish settlers have worked wonders of reclamation in the cool northern regions of Galilee, in the hot waterless plains of the Negev, and in the tropical coastal areas. One of the first great accomplishments of the חֲלוּצִים was the planting of numerous forests.

That is why a special day was set aside to honor עֵצִים. This day is called the רֹאשׁ הַשָּׁנָה לָאִילָנוֹת.

The word Tu is made up of two Hebrew letters, tet and vav. Tet has the numeral value of 9, and vav has the value of 6. Added together they equal 15. The holiday of Tu B'Shevat is celebrated on the 15th day of the month of Shevat.

Land of Promise

Modern יִשְׂרָאֵל grows a great variety of fruits, vegetables, and flowers. Jewish farmers introduced the grapefruit and varieties of oranges into Israel.

Lots of crops, including tobacco, grapes, melons, almonds, pistachio nuts, and pomegranates, to name but a few, show that Israel has truly earned its description as a land of promise.

The Jewish National Fund's best–known task is planting trees. Through the JNF, Jews around the world help plant trees in the Land of Israel. These young forests are often used for recreational purposes. At certain times of the year, such as Tu B'Shevat, Israeli students help with the planting of young saplings, some of which were purchased through donations by other students around the world. Trees are planted to commemorate various occasions: births, anniversaries, a Bar or Bat Mitzvah, graduation. Sad occasions are remembered as well as happy ones.

We Help the JNF

One way we in the United States observe ט״ו בִּשְׁבָט is by contributing to the קֶרֶן קַיֶמֶת לְיִשְׂרָאֵל, which plants young עֵצִים in יִשְׂרָאֵל. These עֵצִים help reclaim for cultivation the earth that has been worn out by centuries of erosion and shifting sand dunes. In less than a century of existence, the קֶרֶן קַיֶמֶת לְיִשְׂרָאֵל has planted millions of עֵצִים and built hundreds of agricultural settlements.

Much of the credit for making Israel bloom as in days of old belongs to the קֶרֶן קַיֶמֶת לְיִשְׂרָאֵל. When the famous עֵמֶק יִזְרָאֵל was bought by the קֶרֶן קַיֶמֶת לְיִשְׂרָאֵל, it was a wasteland, a mass of swamps. Today the Emek is a beautiful valley, studded with orchards and little farms. All this was achieved by the חֲלוּצִים with the help given by Jews everywhere through the קֶרֶן קַיֶמֶת לְיִשְׂרָאֵל.

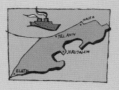

יִשְׂרָאֵל

פֵּרוֹת

It's a Mitzvah 529

ט״ו

כִּי־תָצוּר אֶל־עִיר יָמִים רַבִּים	When you besiege a city for many days
לְהִלָּחֵם עָלֶיהָ לְתָפְשָׂהּ	to capture it
לֹא־תַשְׁחִית אֶת־עֵצָהּ	you shall not destroy the trees
לִנְדֹּחַ עָלָיו גַּרְזֶן.	by using an axe.
כִּי מִמֶּנּוּ תֹאכֵל.	You may eat its fruits.
וְאֹתוֹ לֹא תִכְרֹת.	You must not cut it down,
כִּי הָאָדָם עֵץ הַשָּׂדֶה	because is the tree like a person
לָבֹא מִפָּנֶיךָ בַּמָּצוֹר.	that you should besiege it?

(Devarim 20:19)

ט״ו בִּשְׁבָט is sometimes called the Jewish Arbor Day. In יִשְׂרָאֵל, ט״ו בִּשְׁבָט is observed by planting עֵצִים and eating fruits grown in the land. The Mishnah refers to ט״ו בִּשְׁבָט as רֹאשׁ הַשָּׁנָה לָאִילָנוֹת. In יִשְׂרָאֵל, ט״ו בִּשְׁבָט is celebrated by the planting of saplings and the eating of fruits grown in יִשְׂרָאֵל.
עֵצִים are precious, especially in יִשְׂרָאֵל. The Torah, 5,000 years ago, warned us that it is forbidden to cut down or destroy fruit-bearing עֵצִים or vegetation, even when besieging an enemy city.

עֵץ, עֵצִים

TU B'SHEVAT AT HOME

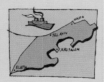

Since ancient times, we have observed the holiday of ט״וּ בִּשְׁבָט by eating fruits grown in יִשְׂרָאֵל. In the sixteenth century the mystics of Safed started the custom of making a ט״וּ בִּשְׁבָט seder, modeled upon the Passsover seder. During the seder, biblical verses that highlight the vegetation of Israel are recited. Four cups of wine are served at the meal as well as a variety of fruits, such as olives, dates, and carobs. It is a mitzvah to eat various types of fruits, and it is a mitzvah to recite the blessings before eating.

As on all special occasions, the blessings are followed by the שֶׁהֶחֱיָנוּ.

BLESSINGS BEFORE EATING FRUIT

בָּרוּךְ אַתָּה יְהֹוָה, אֱלֹהֵינוּ,	Praised are You, Adonai our God,
מֶלֶךְ הָעוֹלָם,	Ruler of the universe,
בּוֹרֵא פְּרִי הָעֵץ.	Creator of the fruit of the tree.
בָּרוּךְ אַתָּה יְהֹוָה, אֱלֹהֵינוּ,	Praised are You, Adonai our God,
מֶלֶךְ הָעוֹלָם,	Ruler of the universe,
שֶׁהֶחֱיָנוּ וְקִיְּמָנוּ	who has kept us alive and well
וְהִגִּיעָנוּ	and enabled us
לַזְּמַן הַזֶּה.	to celebrate this occasion.

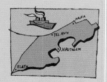

A special ט״וּ בִּשְׁבָט blessing

בָּרוּךְ אַתָּה יהוה,	Praised are You, Adonai,
אֱלֹהֵינוּ מֶלֶךְ הָעוֹלָם,	our God, Ruler of the universe,
שֶׁלֹּא חִסַּר בְּעוֹלָמוֹ דָּבָר,	who left nothing out of Your world,
וּבָרָא בוֹ בְּרִיּוֹת טוֹבוֹת	who has created good creatures
וְאִילָנוֹת טוֹבִים	and healthy trees
לְהָנוֹת בָּהֶם בְּנֵי אָדָם.	for human beings to enjoy.

TU BISHEVAT IN SONG

THE ALMOND TREE

הַשְּׁקֵדִיָּה פּוֹרַחַת,	The almond tree is growing,
וְשֶׁמֶשׁ פָּז זוֹרַחַת,	The golden sun is glowing:
צִפֳּרִים מֵרֹאשׁ כָּל גַּג	The birds sing out in joyous glee
מְבַשְּׂרוֹת אֶת בֹּא הֶחָג.	From every roof and every tree
ט"וּ בִּשְׁבָט הִגִּיעַ,	Tu B'shevat is here,
חַג הָאִילָנוֹת (2).	The holiday of the trees.

THE OLIVE TREES

עֲצֵי זֵיתִים עוֹמְדִים, לַ לַ לַ . . .   The olive trees are standing

TREE PLANTING TIME

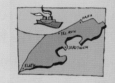

כִּי תָבֹאוּ אֶל הָאָרֶץ	When you shall come into the land
וּנְטַעְתֶּם כָּל עֵץ תְּחִלָּה.	A tree shall be planted first.
וְנָתַן הָעֵץ פִּרְיוֹ	The tree will give of its fruit
וְהָאָרֶץ יְבוּלָהּ.	And the land of its produce

Did You Know?

קֶרֶן קַיֶּמֶת לְיִשְׂרָאֵל
JEWISH NATIONAL FUND

The land for the first settlements in Palestine was purchased by the קֶרֶן קַיֶּמֶת לְיִשְׂרָאֵל **, established in 1901 as the land-purchasing agency of the Zionist movement. The** קֶרֶן קַיֶּמֶת לְיִשְׂרָאֵל **depended on small sums of money collected from Jews throughout the world. The blue and white JNF box found a place in millions of Jewish homes.**

WHY PURIM?

When Israel was part of the Persian Empire, a large community of Jews lived peacefully in the city of Shushan, Persia's capital. הָמָן, the chief officer of King אֲחַשְׁוֵרוֹשׁ, was a very arrogant and wicked man. Drunk with power, he ordered everyone to bow down before him, but the Jew מָרְדְּכַי, who worshipped only God, refused to bow down to הָמָן. הָמָן became very angry at מָרְדְּכַי.

In revenge he decided to destroy all the Jews in Persia. הָמָן persuaded אֲחַשְׁוֵרוֹשׁ that the Jews were a "problem people," and the king gave him a free hand to destroy them.

1 פּוּרִים	Holiday of Lots
2 מְגִלַּת אֶסְתֵּר	A scroll (book of the Bible)
3 שׁוּשָׁן	Susa (Persian city)
4 אֶסְתֵּר	Queen who saved the Jews of Persia
5 הָמָן	Evil Persian noble who wanted to kill Jews
6 אֲחַשְׁוֵרוֹשׁ	King of Persia
7 מָרְדְּכַי	Cousin of Esther

Mordecai Saves the King

One day מָרְדְּכַי overheard a plot to kill the king. He reported the plot and saved the life of King אֲחַשְׁוֵרוֹשׁ. The king then asked הָמָן to advise him how to reward a man who had done the king a great service. הָמָן thought that the king wanted to honor him. He suggested that such a man should be paraded through the streets wearing the king's clothes and riding on the king's horse. Can you imagine the anger of הָמָן after he learned that the man to be honored was his enemy מָרְדְּכַי?

Haman's Evil Plan

The day chosen by the wicked הָמָן for the slaughter of the Jews was the thirteenth of the Hebrew month of Adar.

The palaces of the Persian kings were very large and ornate. Archaeologists at Persepolis have uncovered several stone palaces dating from the time of Darius and Xerxes. This is the Hall of Pillars with its 72 giant pillars. It was large enough to accommodate 10,000 celebrants.

WHY PURIM?

He chose this day by casting פּוּרִים , which means "lots" in Hebrew. Haman set up a special gallows where he looked forward to hanging מָרְדְּכַי . When מָרְדְּכַי heard of the coming doom for the Jewish people he became filled with dread.

Queen Esther Saves the Jews

אֶסְתֵּר , the queen of Persia, was the niece of מָרְדְּכַי , but the king did not know she was Jewish. מָרְדְּכַי urged her to reveal her heritage and tell the king of the wicked plot to kill the Jews. אֶסְתֵּר was afraid, but מָרְדְּכַי explained that the survival of the Jewish people depended on her alone. "Who knows," said the wise מָרְדְּכַי to אֶסְתֵּר , "if it was not for the sake of this moment that your destiny took you to the royal house?" Queen אֶסְתֵּר took the risk.

The Banquet

She invited אֲחַשְׁוֵרוֹשׁ and הָמָן to a banquet. There she told the king about the evil plot to kill the Jewish people, explaining that she too, was a Jewess and that her people were innocent of wrongdoing. The king was furious at הָמָן and his wicked plot. He ordered his servants to hang הָמָן on the very gallows that had been built for מָרְדְּכַי

Moreover, the king appointed מָרְדְּכַי as his new chief officer and honored אֶסְתֵּר , his Jewish queen, above all the other women in the land.

In memory of this event, the fourteenth day of Adar, the day after the pogrom הָמָן had planned for the Jews of Persia, was made into the joyous holiday of פּוּרִים !

 **Did You Know?**

The name פּוּרִים comes from the Hebrew word *pur* which means "lots." מְגִלַת אֶסְתֵּר tells us that " in the month of Nisan, lots (pur) were cast by Haman, to choose the day and the month for a pogrom, and the month of Adar was chosen.

On November 9, 1938, the Nazis staged a nation wide pogrom that became known as Kristallnacht (Crystal Night) because of the many broken windows. Hundreds of synagogues in Germany were set on fire and Jewish businesses were destroyed. Numerous Jews were murdered by organized mobs of Nazis.

אֶסְתֵּר

מָרְדְּכַי

אֲחַשְׁוֵרוֹשׁ

הָמָן

LE'TS CELEBRATE PURIM

The story of פּוּרִים is told in a special book called the מְגִילַת אֶסְתֵּר.
The מְגִילַת אֶסְתֵּר is read in the synagogue on the evening of פּוּרִים, but this is no solemn and serious occasion.
Everyone is merry and full of fun, and a carnival mood prevails. People wear funny masks and dress in costumes. When מְגִילַת אֶסְתֵּר is chanted, the children listen carefully to the reading, for whenever the name of the hated הָמָן is mentioned, they try to drown it out with the racket from their רַעֲשָׁנִים.

		Hebrew Word Bank
פּוּרִים	1	Holiday of Lots
רַעֲשָׁנִים	2	Noisemakers (graggers in Yiddish)
מִשְׁלוֹחַ מָנוֹת	3	Sending portions, gifts, candy
עַדְלאִידַע	4	Hebrew name for Purim carnival
אָזְנֵי הָמָן	5	Purim cakes
אֲדָר	6	Twelfth month of Hebrew calendar
הָמָן	7	Evil Persian noble
מַחֲצִית הַשֶּׁקֶל	8	Half-shekel
מְגִילַת אֶסְתֵּר	9	Scroll of Esther
אֶסְתֵּר	10	Esther
מָרְדְּכַי	11	Mordecai

The Meaning of Purim

פּוּרִים started as a holiday celebrating the delivery of the Jews from הָמָן during the time of the Persian Empire, but it is now much more. It is a festival on which Jews rejoice at God's protection of the Jewish people from any threatened evil. The name הָמָן has come to stand for any enemy of Israel. מָרְדְּכַי is a name for every wise Jewish leader, and אֶסְתֵּר for every Jewish heroine.

פּוּרִים is the merriest holiday of the Jewish year. It is celebrated on the fourteenth of Adar with carnivals, parties, plays, masquerades, מִשְׁלוֹחַ מָנוֹת, eating, drinking, and silliness. It is the one day of the year when silliness and even drunkenness are encouraged. We are told that we are to get so drunk on this day that we cannot tell the difference between the words "blessed be מָרְדְּכַי" and "cursed be הָמָן."

Reading the Megillah

The מְגִילַת אֶסְתֵּר is read in the synagogue on the evening of פּוּרִים.
Although it is a religious service, it is a time for having fun and being rowdy. The behavior that is permitted in the synagogue on פּוּרִים is not allowed at any other time.

Purim is a time for masquerades, puppet shows, reading the Megillah, making a noise with graggers, and eating lots of hamantashen.

Many people come to the synagogue in funny costumes and masks. All the children (and many adults) bring רַעֲשָׁנִים , graggers, special פּוּרִים noisemakers.

As the reader chants the מְגִילַת אֶסְתֵּר in the traditional sing-song trope, everyone listens carefully for the mention of the name of הָמָן. When they hear it, they make as much noise as they can with their graggers . They are trying to blot out the name of הָמָן. And just as Haman's name is blotted out, we hope that all our enemies will be eliminated.

After the service, there is usually a party. All sorts of good things are served. But no פּוּרִים party would be complete without אָזְנֵי הָמָן. These are small three-cornered pastries filled with poppyseeds, prunes, or other fillings. The three-cornered shape, it is said, was because הָמָן wore a three-cornered hat. In Israel, these cakes are called אָזְנֵי הָמָן , which means "Haman's ears." But whatever you call them, or whatever filling is used, they are delicious.

The Carnival

In religious schools across the country, פּוּרִים is a very busy time. It is the time of the yearly carnival. All the classes have been busy for weeks preparing games of chance and skill. On the Sunday before or after פּוּרִים all these games are set up and all the children of the school are invited to play. Usually children come in costume, and prizes are given for the best costume, the funniest costume, the most original costume, and so on. Many children (and their parents) consider פּוּרִים the best Jewish holiday of the year. "It is too bad," they say "that it does not come at least every other week."

It's a Mitzvah D'rabanan

Besides the 613 Torah mitzvot, the sages also established seven more mitzvot, which are known as Mitzvot d'Rabbanan, rabbinical commandments.

Reading and listening to the reading of the מְגִילַת אֶסְתֵּר is one of the seven rabbinical mitzvot. There are three other mitzvot that can be fulfilled on Purim:

1. Gifts to the poor – מַתָּנוֹת לָאֶבְיוֹנִים

2. Gifts to friends – מִשְׁלוֹחַ מָנוֹת

3. A Purim party – סְעוּדָה

מְגִילַת אֶסְתֵּר

אָזְנֵי הָמָן

רַעֲשָׁן

מַסֵּכוֹת

PURIM IN THE SYNAGOGUE

בִּרְכוֹת קֹדֶם הַמְּגִלָּה
BLESSINGS BEFORE READING THE MEGILLAH

בָּרוּךְ אַתָּה יְיָ,
Praised is Adonai,

אֱלֹהֵינוּ מֶלֶךְ הָעוֹלָם,
our God, Ruler of the universe,

אֲשֶׁר קִדְּשָׁנוּ בְּמִצְוֹתָיו
who made us holy with mitzvot

וְצִוָּנוּ עַל מִקְרָא מְגִלָּה.
and commanded us to read the Megillah.

בָּרוּךְ אַתָּה יְיָ,
Praised is Adonai,

אֱלֹהֵינוּ מֶלֶךְ הָעוֹלָם,
our God, Ruler of the universe,

שֶׁעָשָׂה נִסִּים לַאֲבוֹתֵינוּ
who performed miracles for our ancestors

בַּיָּמִים הָהֵם בַּזְּמַן הַזֶּה.
in those days at this time.

בָּרוּךְ אַתָּה יְיָ,
Praised is Adonai,

אֱלֹהֵינוּ מֶלֶךְ הָעוֹלָם,
our God, Ruler of the universe,

שֶׁהֶחֱיָנוּ וְקִיְּמָנוּ
who has kept us alive and well

וְהִגִּיעָנוּ לַזְּמַן הַזֶּה.
and has given us the opportunity to celebrate this happy occasion.

BLESSING AFTER READING THE MEGILLAH

בָּרוּךְ אַתָּה יְיָ אֱלֹהֵינוּ,
Praised are You, Adonai our God,

מֶלֶךְ הָעוֹלָם,
Ruler of the World,

הָרָב אֶת־רִיבֵנוּ,
Who fights our battles,

וְהַדָּן אֶת־דִּינֵנוּ,
Who judges our problems,

וְהַנּוֹקֵם אֶת־נִקְמָתֵנוּ,
Who takes revenge against those who harm us,

וְהַנִּפְרָע לָנוּ מִצָּרֵינוּ,
Who takes revenge against our enemies,

וְהַמְשַׁלֵּם גְּמוּל לְכָל־אֹיְבֵי נַפְשֵׁנוּ.
And punishes our oppressors.

בָּרוּךְ אַתָּה יְיָ,
Praised are You, Adonai,

הַנִּפְרָע לְעַמּוֹ יִשְׂרָאֵל
Who frees the people of Israel

מִכָּל־צָרֵיהֶם
From their oppressors.

הָאֵל הַמּוֹשִׁיעַ.
God the Savior.

PURIM IN THE SYNAGOGUE

עַל הַנִּסִּים FOR THE MIRACLES

**The Al Hanissim prayer appears in the Amidah
and in the Birkat ha–Mazon which is recited during the Purim holiday.**

עַל הַנִּסִּים	For the miracles,
וְעַל הַפֻּרְקָן,	and the salvations,
וְעַל הַגְּבוּרוֹת,	for the brave deeds,
וְעַל הַתְּשׁוּעוֹת,	and for the help,
וְעַל הַמִּלְחָמוֹת	and for the battles
שֶׁעָשִׂיתָ לַאֲבוֹתֵינוּ	which you fought for our ancestors
בַּיָּמִים הָהֵם	in those long ago times
בִּזְמַן הַזֶּה.	at this of year.
בִּימֵי מָרְדְּכַי וְאֶסְתֵּר	In the days of Mordechai and Esther
בְּשׁוּשַׁן הַבִּירָה	in Shushan, the capital [of Persia],
כְּשֶׁעָמַד עֲלֵיהֶם הָמָן הָרָשָׁע	When evil Haman rose up against them,
בִּקֵּשׁ לְהַשְׁמִיד לַהֲרוֹג	he wanted to destroy, to kill,
וּלְאַבֵּד אֶת כָּל הַיְּהוּדִים,	and to murder all the Jews,
מִנַּעַר וְעַד זָקֵן, טַף וְנָשִׁים,	young and old, infants and women,
בְּיוֹם אֶחָד, בִּשְׁלֹשָׁה עָשָׂר	on one day, the thirteenth day
לְחֹדֶשׁ שְׁנֵים עָשָׂר,	of the twelfth month,
הוּא חֹדֶשׁ אֲדָר,	which is the month of Adar,
וּשְׁלָלָם לָבוֹז.	and to steal all their property.
וְאַתָּה בְּרַחֲמֶיךָ הָרַבִּים	You, in Your abundant mercy
הֵפַרְתָּ אֶת עֲצָתוֹ,	defeated his counsel,
וְקִלְקַלְתָּ אֶת מַחֲשַׁבְתּוֹ,	frustrated his intention,
וַהֲשֵׁבוֹתָ לּוֹ גְּמוּלוֹ בְּרֹאשׁוֹ,	and brought his evil plan upon his own head,
וְתָלוּ אוֹתוֹ וְאֶת בָּנָיו	and they hanged him and his sons
עַל הָעֵץ.	upon the gallows.

PURIM IN SONG

שׁוֹשַׁנַּת יַעֲקֹב
THE FLOWER OF JACOB

This פּוּרִים song tells how the Jews were saved by Queen אֶסְתֵּר and how הָמָן and his anti-Semitic allies were defeated.

שׁוֹשַׁנַּת יַעֲקֹב	The "Shushan Jews" (flower of Jacob)
צָהֲלָה וְשָׂמֵחָה	shouted with joy
בִּרְאוֹתָם יַחַד תְּכֵלֶת	when they saw Mordechai dressed in
מָרְדְּכָי.	royal purple.

The song then thanks God for having saved the Jews.

תְּשׁוּעָתָם הָיִיתָ לָנֶצַח	You were always their salvation
וְתִקְוָתָם בְּכָל דּוֹר וָדוֹר.	and their hope in every generation.
לְהוֹדִיעַ שֶׁכָּל קֹוֶיךָ	To tell that those who have hope in You will
לֹא יֵבוֹשׁוּ,	not be shamed,
וְלֹא יִכָּלְמוּ לָנֶצַח	those who seek refuge in You shall never
כָּל הַחוֹסִים בָּךְ.	be disappointed.

Finally, using familiar phrases, the idea of פּוּרִים is stated in a nutshell.

אָרוּר הָמָן,	Cursed is Haman,
אֲשֶׁר בִּקֵּשׁ לְאַבְּדִי.	who tried to make me perish.
בָּרוּךְ מָרְדְּכַי הַיְּהוּדִי.	Praised is Mordechai the Jew.

PURIM IN SONG

חַג פּוּרִים PURIM HOLIDAY

חַג פּוּרִים, חַג פּוּרִים — Purim holiday, Purim holiday –

חַג גָּדוֹל הוּא לַיְּהוּדִים. A great holiday for all the Jews.

מַסֵּכוֹת, רַעֲשָׁנִים, Masks, noisemakers,

זְמִירוֹת וְרִקּוּדִים. Songs and dance.

הָבָה נַרְעִישָׁה Lets make noise

רַשׁ, רַשׁ, רַשׁ, Rash, rash, rash,

בָּרַעֲשָׁנִים. With our graggers.

Purim Commentary

Anti–Semites have always hated the מְגִילָה, and the Nazis forbade its reading in the concentration camps. Before their deaths, Jewish inmates of Auschwitz, Dachau, and Treblinka wrote copies of the מְגִילָה from memory and read it in secret on פּוּרִים. Their enemies understood its message. In every age martyrs as well as ordinary men and women have seen it as a record of deliverance and a prophecy of future victory.

WHY PASSOVER?

During a time of famine in Canaan, the family of Jacob (Israel) consisted of 72 people. The בְּנֵי יִשְׂרָאֵל settled in the land of Goshen in מִצְרַיִם. For years they lived in peace and prosperity, but suddenly everything changed. A new פַּרְעֹה enslaved the בְּנֵי יִשְׂרָאֵל. Pharaoh ordered all their newborn sons killed!

The Birth of Moses

An Israelite woman named Yocheved hid her newborn son, מֹשֶׁה, in a sealed basket and placed it among the Nile's reeds. The princess of Egypt found the baby and raised him in the royal palace. מֹשֶׁה learned from his mother, Yocheved, that he was a Jew. After killing an Egyptian taskmaster who had been mercilessly beating a Jewish slave, מֹשֶׁה fled to the wilderness of Midian. One day מֹשֶׁה saw a burning bush. When he came closer, he heard the voice of God, who told him to go down to מִצְרַיִם and lead the Hebrew slaves to freedom.

HEBREW WORD BANK

פֶּסַח	1	Passover
זְמַן חֵרוּתֵינוּ	2	Season of Our Freedom
מַכּוֹת	3	Plagues
פַּרְעֹה	4	King of Egypt who enslaved the Hebrew
מֹשֶׁה	5	Moses, the leader and prophet of Israel
אַהֲרֹן	6	Aaron, the brother of Moses
מִצְרַיִם	7	Egypt
חַג הַפֶּסַח	8	Holiday of the Paschal lamb
חַג הָאָסִיף	9	Holiday of ingathering
חַג הַמַּצוֹת	10	Holiday of matzot
חַג הָאָבִיב	11	Holiday of spring
בְּנֵי יִשְׂרָאֵל	12	Children of Israel

The Ten Plagues

מֹשֶׁה tried to do as God commanded, but פַּרְעֹה just laughed. Frightful מַכּוֹת began to happen because of his refusal to let the Hebrew slaves go. All the water of מִצְרַיִם turned to blood.

The Israelite slaves made bricks out of clay, mud, and straw. The straw which the taskmasters supplied held the bricks together. The Torah says that Pharaoh wanted to punish the Israelites and ordered them to find their own straw.

In some poor Middle Eastern countries, peasants still build their houses out of sunbaked bricks, just as the Israelites did thousands of years ago. This peasant is setting his mud bricks out to dry in the hot sun. Note the straw strewn around the pile of bricks.

Frogs swarmed over the country. Insects attacked the crops. Darkness, even in the daytime, cast everyone into confusion, but still the stubborn פַּרְעֹה refused to let the בְּנֵי יִשְׂרָאֵל leave.

The last מַכּוֹת was the worst of all. All the firstborn children of מִצְרַיִם died, but the firstborn children of the בְּנֵי יִשְׂרָאֵל were left unharmed—"passed over." This is the source of the name Passover—פֶּסַח in Hebrew.

משֶׁה

The Miracle at the Red Sea

פַּרְעֹה finally released the בְּנֵי יִשְׂרָאֵל. The people of מִצְרַיִם were so anxious to see the end of the terrible מַכּוֹת that they rushed the former slaves out of the land. But once the בְּנֵי יִשְׂרָאֵל were gone, פַּרְעֹה changed his mind. He sent his army to recapture them. The Egyptians caught up with the בְּנֵי יִשְׂרָאֵל at the Red Sea. Then God miraculously divided the waters so that the בְּנֵי יִשְׂרָאֵל could pass through safely. The chariots of פַּרְעֹה charged after them, but the waters closed again, drowning the Egyptians, and the בְּנֵי יִשְׂרָאֵל were saved.

אַהֲרֹן

The Meaning of Passover

Each year, on the fifteenth day of Nisan, we begin the celebration of פֶּסַח. This holiday reminds us of the escape from slavery in מִצְרַיִם. With the Exodus ("going-out") from מִצְרַיִם, the בְּנֵי יִשְׂרָאֵל came together as people and readied themselves to accept God's Torah. פֶּסַח always comes in the springtime. פֶּסַח has four different names. It is known as the חַג הָאָבִיב, because it marks the beginning of springtime. It is also known as חַג הָאָסִיף because it was also harvest time.

In ancient days on פֶּסַח, the בְּנֵי יִשְׂרָאֵל would make a pilgrimage to the Holy Temple in Jerusalem, bringing sheaves of barley, known as omer as gifts.

פַּרְעֹה

When God appointed משֶׁה to lead the people out of מִצְרַיִם, they left so quickly that they did not have time to bake their bread. The bread became מַצּוֹת because there was no time for the dough to rise. That is why פֶּסַח is also called חַג הַמַצוֹת.

Finally פֶּסַח is called זְמַן חֵרוּתֵינוּ, because it honors the great blessing of freedom won by the Israelites.

מִצְרַיִם

LET'S CELEBRATE PASSOVER

The long cold winter is over. Spring has come. The leaves on the trees are beginning to turn green. The spring flowers are beginning to push through the earth. The air is warm and relaxed. The whole world seems happy and glad to be alive.

Everyone is getting ready for פֶּסַח, which is celebrated for eight days beginning on the fifteenth of Nisan. פֶּסַח is the holiday of spring, the Festival of Freedom, the Holiday of Matzot.

The days just before פֶּסַח are one of the busiest times of the year.

All chametz (anything made with flour) must be put away. Foods must be cooked, and all the preparations for the סֵדֶר must be made.

The Seder

The סֵדֶר is the highlight of the פֶּסַח season.
It is a complete service that takes place at home with family and guests seated around the table. The table is set in a special way and special rituals are followed.

In the center of the table is the קְעָרָה, or סֵדֶר plate. On it are מָרוֹר, a shankbone, a mixture of apples, nuts, and wine called חֲרוֹסֶת, a roasted egg, and a green vegetable, such as parsley or celery. Each one of these foods stand for something important. The מָרוֹר stands for the bitterness of slavery.

The seder leader gets ready to break the middle matzah and prepare the afikomen.

אֵלִיָּהוּ

The shankbone reminds us of the Paschal lamb that the Israelites ate at their last meal in Egypt. The חֲרוֹסֶת looks like the mortar the Children of Israel used in Egypt to make bricks. The roasted egg stands for the special holiday sacrifice Jews made on all holidays at the Temple in Jerusalem. The karpas, or parsley, represents spring and the new life this season brings to the earth. It is dipped in salt water to remind the Jews of the tears they shed as slaves in Egypt.

אֲפִיקוֹמָן

Matzah and Wine

In the center of the table is a tray on which there are three whole מַצּוֹת covered with a cloth. Many families now add a fourth מַצָּה which they call the מַצָּה of Hope. This fourth מַצָּה helps us to remember that there are still Jews who live in countries where they are not free and cannot celebrate פֶּסַח as they would like to.
Four times during the סֵדֶר the glass will be filled with wine, the blessing for wine will be recited, and the wine will be drunk.
In front of each person is a הַגָּדָה, the book that contains the rituals for the סֵדֶר. The word הַגָּדָה means "telling," and the הַגָּדָה tells us exactly what we are supposed to do. It also tells us the story of פֶּסַח.

קְעָרָה

מַצָּה

It's a Mitzvah 21

וְהִגַּדְתָּ לְבִנְךָ   And you shall tell your child

בַּיּוֹם הַהוּא   on that day

Shemot 13:8

It is a mitzvah for you to participate in a סֵדֶר and to retell the story of the Exodus from Egypt.

הַגָּדָה

The Order of the Seder

The Hebrew word סֵדֶר means "order." It refers to the order in which things take place at the פֶּסַח meal. It is very easy to learn how to make a סֵדֶר. Even those who have never done it before can follow the instructions in the הַגָּדָה. The same order is used all over the world.

ORDER OF THE PASSOVER SEDER

1. Recite the Kiddush. קַדֵּשׁ.
2. Wash the hands וּרְחַץ.
3. Eat a green vegetable. כַּרְפַּס.
4. Break the middle מַצָּה, hide half for the אֲפִיקוֹמָן. יַחַץ.
5. Recite the פֶּסַח story. מַגִּיד.
6. Wash your hands before the meal. רָחְצָה.
7. Say Hamotzi and the special blessing for the מַצָּה. מוֹצִיא מַצָּה.
8. Eat the מָרוֹר. מָרוֹר.
9. Eat the מַצָּה and מָרוֹר together. כּוֹרֵךְ.
10. Serve the פֶּסַח meal. שֻׁלְחָן עוֹרֵךְ.
11. Eat the אֲפִיקוֹמָן. צָפוּן.
12. Recite the grace after the meal. בָּרֵךְ.
13. Recite the Hallel. הַלֵּל.
14. End the סֵדֶר. נִרְצָה.

The Four Questions

One of the highlights for children of the סֵדֶר is the asking of the אַרְבַּע קוּשִׁיוֹת. The answers to the אַרְבַּע קוּשִׁיוֹת tells the story of פֶּסַח.

Four Cups of Wine

Everyone at the סֵדֶר table drinks אַרְבַּע כּוֹסוֹת, in the order mentioned in the הַגָּדָה. There are אַרְבַּע כּוֹסוֹת because in the Torah, God as promise to free the Israelites from slavery is repeated four times.

Every person at the seder drinks אַרְבַּע כּוֹסוֹת. But a fifth cup of wine is also poured. Known as the כּוֹס אֵלִיָּהוּ, it honors the prophet Elijah. You open your door for Elijah the prophet, to show that you are free and that you and your people are celebrating Passover for all the world to see.

The Bible tells us that Elijah did many wonderful and miraculous deeds. According to one of the legends, Elijah will come back to earth, and when he does, it will be the beginning of a golden age. The whole world will be at peace, and we will all love one another.

אֵלִיָּהוּ

אֲפִיקוֹמָן

קְעָרָה

מַצָּה

הַגָּדָה

Ani Ma'amin

In some homes, a new ceremony has been introduced before the door is opened for the prophet Elijah. During the ceremony, we remember the six million Jews who were murdered by the Nazis and the heroes of the ghetto revolts.

We sing the song "Ani Ma'amin". This song of hope was sung by the martyrs in the concentration camps.

The words were written in accordance with the teaching of the famous Jewish philosopher Moses Maimonides.

אֵלִיָּהוּ

אֲנִי מַאֲמִין בֶּאֱמוּנָה שְׁלֵמָה	I believe with complete faith
בְּבִיאַת הַמָּשִׁיחַ.	in the coming of the Messianic age of peace.
וְאַף עַל פִּי שֶׁיִּתְמַהְמֵהַּ,	And though it takes a long time to arrive,
עִם כָּל־זֶה אֲחַכֶּה לוֹ	I will still wait.
בְּכָל־יוֹם שֶׁיָּבֹא.	Until it is here.

אֲפִיקוֹמֶן

That is the story of פֶּסַח, a heroic revolt against oppression and a glorious freedom from slavery. Throughout the ages, פֶּסַח has symbolized freedom: whether escape from Egypt, rescue from the Crusaders of the Middle Ages, or liberation from the Nazis.

Just as we overcame our enemies in the land of Egypt, so will the Jewish people always vanquish its oppressors. That is the message of פֶּסַח.

קְעָרָה

מַצָּה

THE TEN PLAGUES

Pharaoh refused to let the Israelites leave Egypt, so God punished Egypt with ten plagues. After the tenth plague Pharaoh permitted the Israelites to leave.

1. BLOOD— דָּם.

2. FROGS— צְפַרְדֵּעַ. 3. LICE— כִּנִּים. 4. FLIES— עָרוֹב.

5. CATTLE DISEASE— דֶּבֶר. 6. BOILS— שְׁחִין. 7. HAIL— בָּרָד.

8. LOCUSTS— אַרְבֶּה. 9. DARKNESS— חֹשֶׁךְ. 10. SLAYING OF FIRSTBORN— מַכַּת בְּכֹרוֹת.

הַגָּדָה

PASSOVER AT HOME

הַדְלָקַת הַגֵּרוֹת לְחַג הַמַּצוֹת
PASSOVER CANDLE LIGHTING PRAYER

In the beginning of the universe, Adonai said, "Let there be light." That is the mission of Judaism: to kindle the light of justice and destroy the darkness of hate. When you light the פֶּסַח candles, you become Adonai's co-creators and pray, "Let there be light, and let there be peace."

בָּרוּךְ אַתָּה יְיָ,	Praised is Adonai,
אֱלֹהֵינוּ מֶלֶךְ הָעוֹלָם,	our God, Ruler of the universe,
אֲשֶׁר קִדְּשָׁנוּ בְּמִצְוֹתָיו	who made us holy by the mitzvot
וְצִוָּנוּ לְהַדְלִיק נֵר שֶׁל יוֹם טוֹב.	by commanding us to light candles on the festival.
בָּרוּךְ אַתָּה יְיָ,	Praised is Adonai,
אֱלֹהֵינוּ מֶלֶךְ הָעוֹלָם,	our God, Ruler of the universe,
שֶׁהֶחֱיָנוּ וְקִיְּמָנוּ	who has kept us alive and well
וְהִגִּיעָנוּ לַזְּמַן הַזֶּה.	and has given us the opportunity to celebrate this occasion.

It's a Mitzvah 302

מָעוֹת חִטִּים
MONEY FOR WHEAT

Tzedakah means "charity." We do tzedakah when we help the poor and those who cannot help themselves.

Right after the holiday of Purim the synagogues and the temples begin collecting tzedakah for the holiday of פֶּסַח.

The special tzedakah money is called מָעוֹת חִטִּים ("money for wheat")

Years ago מָעוֹת חִטִּים money was used to buy wheat. This wheat was baked into מַצָּה for poor people.

82

PASSOVER AT HOME

The Passover Kiddush emphasizes three aspects of the holiday:
1. Holiday of matzot 2. Holiday of freedom 3. Exodus from Egypt.

וַיְהִי־עֶרֶב, וַיְהִי־בֹקֶר, יוֹם הַשִּׁשִּׁי.	It was evening and morning on the sixth day.
וַיְכֻלּוּ הַשָּׁמַיִם וְהָאָרֶץ וְכָל־צְבָאָם.	The universe and planet earth and all that was within them had been completed.
וַיְכַל אֱלֹהִים בַּיּוֹם הַשְּׁבִיעִי, מְלַאכְתּוֹ אֲשֶׁר עָשָׂה,	Elohim finished all the work of creation by the seventh day,
וַיִּשְׁבֹּת בַּיּוֹם הַשְּׁבִיעִי	And Elohim rested on the seventh day
מִכָּל מְלַאכְתּוֹ אֲשֶׁר עָשָׂה.	from doing all the work of creation.
וַיְבָרֶךְ אֱלֹהִים אֶת־יוֹם הַשְּׁבִיעִי וַיְקַדֵּשׁ אֹתוֹ,	And Elohim blessed the seventh day and made it holy,
כִּי בוֹ שָׁבַת מִכָּל מְלַאכְתּוֹ	because then Elohim rested from
אֲשֶׁר בָּרָא אֱלֹהִים לַעֲשׂוֹת.	all the work of creation.

If the holiday begins on a weekday, start here.

בָּרוּךְ אַתָּה יְיָ,	Praised is Adonai,
אֱלֹהֵינוּ מֶלֶךְ הָעוֹלָם,	our God, Ruler of the universe,
בּוֹרֵא פְּרִי הַגָּפֶן.	who created the fruit of the vine.
בָּרוּךְ אַתָּה יְיָ,	Praised is Adonai,
אֱלֹהֵינוּ מֶלֶךְ הָעוֹלָם,	our God, Ruler of the universe,
אֲשֶׁר בָּחַר בָּנוּ מִכָּל־עָם,	who chose us from among all people,
וְרוֹמְמָנוּ מִכָּל־לָשׁוֹן,	and raised us from among all other languages,
וְקִדְּשָׁנוּ בְּמִצְוֹתָיו.	and made us holy with commandments,
וַתִּתֶּן־לָנוּ, יְיָ אֱלֹהֵינוּ, בְּאַהֲבָה (שַׁבָּתוֹת לִמְנוּחָה),	and in love, gave us (Shabbats of rest),
מוֹעֲדִים לְשִׂמְחָה,	festivals of joy,
חַגִּים וּזְמַנִּים לְשָׂשׂוֹן,	and special days of gladness.

continued on page 84

אֶת־יוֹם חַג הַמַּצוֹת הַזֶּה,
the holiday of matzot,

זְמַן חֵרוּתֵנוּ.
the time of freedom.

(בְּאַהֲבָה) מִקְרָא קֹדֶשׁ,
You gave us (in love) this holy event,
so, that we may remember our Exodus,

זֵכֶר לִיצִיאַת מִצְרָיִם.
from Egypt.

כִּי בָנוּ בָחַרְתָּ, וְאוֹתָנוּ קִדַּשְׁתָּ,
You have chosen us and made us holy

מִכָּל הָעַמִּים
among all the nations

(וְשַׁבָּת) וּמוֹעֲדֵי קָדְשֶׁךָ, (בְּאַהֲבָה וּבְרָצוֹן)
And You gave us Your holy days of joy (and

בְּשִׂמְחָה וּבְשָׂשׂוֹן הִנְחַלְתָּנוּ.
Your Shabbat with love).

בָּרוּךְ אַתָּה יְיָ,
Praised is Adonai,

מְקַדֵּשׁ (הַשַּׁבָּת,
who makes holy (Shabbat),

וְ)יִשְׂרָאֵל וְהַזְּמַנִּים.
Israel, and all the seasons.

בָּרוּךְ אַתָּה יְהֹוָה, אֱלֹהֵינוּ,
Praised are You, Adonai our God,

מֶלֶךְ הָעוֹלָם,
Ruler of the universe,

שֶׁהֶחֱיָנוּ וְקִיְּמָנוּ
who has kept us alive and well

וְהִגִּיעָנוּ
and enabled us

לַזְּמַן הַזֶּה.
to celebrate this occasion.

PASSOVER AT HOME

הָא לַחְמָא עַנְיָא THIS IS THE MATZAH OF BITTERNESS

THE SEDER STARTS

The custom of inviting all who are hungry to come and eat originated in Babylonia. Therefore, the invitation is extended in Aramaic, the everyday language spoken by the Jewish people who lived there. Today, a special fund called מְעוֹת חִטִּים, meaning "Money for Wheat ," distributes money so that the poor can enjoy their own סֵדֶר without degrading themselves by begging. Passover is not the only holiday when Jews participate in the mitzvah of helping the poor and the underprivileged.

הָא לַחְמָא עַנְיָא	This is the matzah of bitterness
דִּי אֲכַלוּ אַבְהָתַנָא	Which our ancestors ate
בְּאַרְעָא דְמִצְרָיִם.	in the Land of Egypt.
כָּל דִּכְפִין יֵיתֵי וְיֵכֹל,	Let all who are hungry come and eat,
כָּל דִּצְרִיךְ יֵיתֵי וְיִפְסַח.	Let all who are needy come and celebrate the seder with us.
הַשַּׁתָּא הָכָא,	Now we are here,
לְשָׁנָה הַבָּאָה בְּאַרְעָא דְיִשְׂרָאֵל.	Next year may we be in the Land of Israel.
הַשַּׁתָּא עַבְדֵי,	This year we are like slaves,
לְשָׁנָה הַבָּאָה בְּנֵי חוֹרִין.	Next year may we be free people.

It's a Mitzvah 302

בָּרִאשֹׁן	In the first month
בְּאַרְבָּעָה עָשָׂר יוֹם לַחֹדֶשׁ	From the fourteenth day of the month
בָּעֶרֶב	At evening
תֹּאכְלוּ מַצֹּת	You shall eat matzot
עַד יוֹם הָאֶחָד וְעֶשְׂרִים	Until the twenty-first day
לַחֹדֶשׁ בָּעָרֶב.	Of the month in the evening.

Shemot 12:18

The Torah tells us that it is a mitzvah to start eating מַצָּה on the evening of the fifteenth day of Nisan. We eat מַצָּה on פֶּסַח because the Israelites left in such a hurry in the middle of the night that they had no time to leaven their dough. So they strapped the raw dough to their kneading trays and began their march to freedom.
The hot desert sun baked the raw, unleavened dough into מַצָּה .

מַה נִּשְׁתַּנָּה

The ancients designed the סֵדֶר as a historical, religious, and teaching holiday. The הַגָּדָה contains a variety of teaching techniques, such as stories, songs, rituals, and questions and answers. The אַרְבַּע קוּשִׁיוֹת is a question–and–answer learning and teaching excercise.

מַה נִּשְׁתַּנָּה	Why is
הַלַּיְלָה הַזֶּה	this night different
מִכָּל הַלֵּילוֹת?	from all other nights?
1) שֶׁבְּכָל הַלֵּילוֹת	1. On all other nights
אָנוּ אוֹכְלִין חָמֵץ וּמַצָּה.	we eat either leavened bread or matzah.
הַלַּיְלָה הַזֶּה כֻּלּוֹ מַצָּה.	On this night we only eat matzah.
2) שֶׁבְּכָל הַלֵּילוֹת	2. On all other nights
אָנוּ אוֹכְלִין שְׁאָר יְרָקוֹת.	we eat all kinds of herbs.
הַלַּיְלָה הַזֶּה כֻּלּוֹ מָרוֹר.	On this night, only bitter herbs.
3) שֶׁבְּכָל הַלֵּילוֹת	3. On all other nights
אֵין אָנוּ מַטְבִּילִין	we do not dip
אֲפִילוּ פַּעַם אֶחָת.	even once.
הַלַּיְלָה הַזֶּה שְׁתֵּי פְעָמִים.	On this night, we dip twice.
4) שֶׁבְּכָל הַלֵּילוֹת	4. On all other nights
אָנוּ אוֹכְלִין	we eat
בֵּין יוֹשְׁבִין וּבֵין מְסֻבִּין.	sitting or reclining.
הַלַּיְלָה הַזֶּה כֻּלָּנוּ מְסֻבִּין.	On this night we all eat reclining in a festive manner.

Did You Know?

At the סֵדֶר we observe several ceremonies that involve the number four

4
questions
children
cups of wine

PASSOVER AT HOME

The next four blessings are an important part of the סֵדֶר **ritual.**

Before we eat the karpas we say:

בָּרוּךְ אַתָּה יְיָ,
אֱלֹהֵינוּ מֶלֶךְ הָעוֹלָם,
בּוֹרֵא פְּרִי הָאֲדָמָה.

Praised is Adonai,
our God, Ruler of the universe,
who created produce of the soil.

Before we eat the מָרוֹר **we say:**

בָּרוּךְ אַתָּה יְיָ,
אֱלֹהֵינוּ מֶלֶךְ הָעוֹלָם,
אֲשֶׁר קִדְּשָׁנוּ בְּמִצְוֹתָיו
וְצִוָּנוּ עַל אֲכִילַת מָרוֹר.

Praised is Adonai,
our God, Ruler of the universe,
who made us holy with mitzvot
and commanded us to eat bitter herbs.

Before we eat the מַצָּה **we recite these two blessings:**

בָּרוּךְ אַתָּה יְיָ,
אֱלֹהֵינוּ מֶלֶךְ הָעוֹלָם,
הַמּוֹצִיא לֶחֶם מִן הָאָרֶץ.

Praised is Adonai,
our God, Ruler of the universe,
who brings forth food
from the earth.

בָּרוּךְ אַתָּה יְיָ,
אֱלֹהֵינוּ מֶלֶךְ הָעוֹלָם,
אֲשֶׁר קִדְּשָׁנוּ בְּמִצְוֹתָיו
וְצִוָּנוּ עַל אֲכִילַת מַצָּה.

Praised is Adonai,
our God, Ruler of the universe,
who made us holy with mitzvot
and commanded us to eat matzah.

PASSOVER AT HOME

During the סֵדֶר you sing these songs.

דַּיֵּנוּ

אִלּוּ הוֹצִיאָנוּ מִמִּצְרַיִם,	If the Eternal had just brought us out of Egypt,
דַּיֵּנוּ.	Dayenu – It would have been enough.
אִלּוּ נָתַן לָנוּ אֶת הַשַּׁבָּת,	If the Eternal had just given us the Shabbat,
דַּיֵּנוּ.	Dayenu – It would have been enough.
אִלּוּ נָתַן לָנוּ אֶת הַתּוֹרָה,	If the Eternal had just given us the Torah,
דַּיֵּנוּ.	Dayenu – It would have been enough.

אַדִּיר הוּא

אַדִּיר הוּא,	The Eternal is mighty,
יִבְנֶה בֵּיתוֹ בְּקָרוֹב.	May the Temple be rebuilt.
בִּמְהֵרָה,	Speedily, speedily,
בִּמְהֵרָה בְּיָמֵינוּ בְּקָרוֹב.	In our lifetime – very soon.
אֵל בְּנֵה, אֵל בְּנֵה,	O Eternal, O Eternal,
בְּנֵה בֵּיתְךָ בְּקָרוֹב.	Rebuild Your temple soon.

אֶחָד מִי יוֹדֵעַ?

אֶחָד מִי יוֹדֵעַ, ?	Who knows one?
אֶחָד אֲנִי יוֹדֵעַ.	I know one.
אֶחָד אֱלֹהֵינוּ	One is our God
שֶׁבַּשָּׁמַיִם וּבָאָרֶץ.	In heaven and on earth.

חַד גַּדְיָא   **ONE LITTLE GOAT**

חַד גַּדְיָא, חַד גַּדְיָא.	Chad Gadya, Chad Gadya. One little goat.
דְּזַבִּין אַבָּא בִּתְרֵי זוּזֵי,	One that my parents bought for two zuzim,
חַד גַּדְיָא, חַד גַּדְיָא.	Chad Gadya, Chad Gadya.

יְרוּשָׁלַיִם.

לְשָׁנָה הַבָּאָה בִּירוּשָׁלַיִם.   Next year in Jerusalem.

PASSOVER AT HOME

נִרְצָה
CONCLUSION OF THE SEDER

We end the סֵדֶר with the Hebrew words,

"Next year in Jerusalem" :לְשָׁנָה הַבָּאָה בִּירוּשָׁלָיִם

Our people began in the Land of Israel thousands of years ago. Our people loved the Land of Israel. They used to say that Israel was the center of the world, and right in the middle of Israel was Jerusalem and the Holy Temple. But almost 2,000 years ago most of the Jews were driven out of Israel. Then in 1948, after much fighting, the State of Israel was set up again. Once again Israel is free. Once again the holy city of Jerusalem is the capital of Israel.

חֲסַל סִדּוּר פֶּסַח כְּהִלְכָתוֹ,	The seder is ended,
כְּכָל מִשְׁפָּטוֹ וְחֻקָּתוֹ.	According to custom and law.
כַּאֲשֶׁר זָכִינוּ לְסַדֵּר אוֹתוֹ,	As we were worthy to celebrate it this year,
כֵּן נִזְכֶּה לַעֲשׂוֹתוֹ.	So may we perform it in future years.
זַךְ שׁוֹכֵן מְעוֹנָה,	O Pure One in heaven above,
קוֹמֵם קְהַל עֲדַת מִי מָנָה.	Speedily lead Your redeemed People.
בְּקָרוֹב נַהֵל נִטְעֵי כַנָּה,	Restore the people of Israel in Your love
פְּדוּיִם לְצִיּוֹן בְּרִנָּה.	To Zion in joy.
לְשָׁנָה הַבָּאָה בִּירוּשָׁלָיִם:	NEXT YEAR IN JERUSALEM

All Sing
לְשָׁנָה הַבָּאָה בִּירוּשָׁלָיִם:

WHY YOM HA-SHOAH?

On יוֹם הַשּׁוֹאָה we think of the bravery of the six million Jewish men, women, and children whose lives were viciously snuffed out by the cruelty of the Nazis while the world looked on in silence.

The Warsaw Ghetto Uprising

When the Nazis marched into וַרְשָׁה in October 1939, they found 360,000 Jews in the city. They erected an eight-foot wall around הַגֶּטוֹ בְּוַרְשָׁה and began to ship Jews to the מַחֲנֵה רִכּוּז. Within two years, only 40,000 Jews were left in וַרְשָׁה. The survivors formed the Jewish Fighters Organization, led by twenty-three-year-old Mordecai Anielewicz. Arms were smuggled in, and training sessions were held at night. The first real test came on January 18, 1943. Nazi troops marched into הַגֶּטוֹ בְּוַרְשָׁה to round up a batch of Jews for deportation. They were met by a hail of bullets and by bombs hurled by Jewish fighters disguised in German uniforms.

YOM HA-SHOAH יוֹם הַשּׁוֹאָה

The Final Attack

On April 19, the final attack began. Nazi units marched in. Suddenly a bomb fell on the leading tank. It had been thrown by a girl and it signaled the counterattack. Blue and white flags appeared on roofs. Posters on shattered walls declared:

"We will fight to the last drop of blood!"

The Jews had only one possible goal left—to make the German victory as shameful as possible. Each defender took several Nazis with him when he died.

Mordecai Anielewicz helped organize the revolt against the Nazis in the Warsaw Ghetto. He died fighting the Germans. This statue in memory of Mordecai Anielewicz is at Kibbutz Yad Mordecai in Israel. The water tower was destroyed by Egyptian shells during the War of Independence in 1948.

The Righteous Gentiles

During the שׁוֹאָה, there were many non-Jews (gentiles) who risked their lives to save Jews from the Nazis. These righteous non-Jews are called חֲסִידֵי הָאוּמוֹת.

נֵר זִכָּרוֹן

The Righteous Gentiles of Le Chambon

In France, the 2,500 people who lived in the village of Le Chambon saved about 2,000 Jews. The Jewish refugees found shelter among the villagers. Le Chambon became known as "the nest of the Jews." Although the people of Le Chambon lived in fear, not one person among the 2,500 villagers informed the Nazis.

יְרוּשָׁלַיִם

Raoul Wallenberg

Raoul Wallenberg, a Swedish diplomat in Hungary, issued false passports that saved thousands of Jews. Wallenberg was captured by the Russians and disappeared. To this day nobody is certain what happened to him.

מַחֲנֶה רִכּוּז

Oskar Schindler

Oskar Schindler was an ethnic German born in Czechoslovakia. Toward the end of 1939 he arrived in Cracow, Poland, and took over an enamelware factory that had belonged to Jews.
It had 900 Jewish employees. Schindler persuaded the Nazis to transform his plant into a munitions plant for the war. He insisted, "I need the Jews because of their skills."
Thanks to Schindler's humane efforts, most of the workers at his factory survived. Schindler himself said, "I hated the Nazis and could not see people destroyed. I did what my conscience told me I must do." More than 1,200 Jews were saved by this brave man.

LET'S OBSERVE YOM HA-SHOAH

It is almost unbearable to think about the שׁוֹאָה, the most terrible event in Jewish history. Six million Jews were killed between the years 1939 and 1945, for no other reason than that they were Jews.

Innocent men, women, and children were cruelly beaten, tortured, and killed in the ghettos and the מַחֲנֵי רְכּוּז.

Six million Jews. The number is so big that it is hard to imagine.

Why We Must Never Forget

The events of the שׁוֹאָה are so horrible that we feel like crying when we think about them. But as much as we would like to forget the שׁוֹאָה, we must remember it. We must keep every pain-filled memory alive, so that we never allow

something so awful to happen ever again. יוֹם הַשּׁוֹאָה, the Holocaust Remembrance Day, is observed in Israel and the world over on the twenty-seventh day of נִיסָן. On this day, we remember the six million helpless victims of the Nazis, and we remember those who courageously resisted their attackers, even if only for a few proud days.

Yom Ha–Shoah in Israel

On יוֹם הַשּׁוֹאָה, a siren brings all Israel to a halt. For a moment, everyone in the country stops whatever he or she is doing, stands up quietly, and remembers. We force ourselves to remember all the terror and horror. We relive every wound of body and of spirit, and we vow never to let another שׁוֹאָה take place.

At the יָד-וָשֵׁם in יְרוּשָׁלַיִם, special ceremonies are held. At this center, eternal candles flicker in the dimness, marking our remembrance of those who died in the שׁוֹאָה.

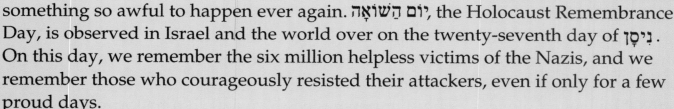

The Yad Vashem Memorial: Ohel Yizkor–Hall of Remembrance. The walls are built of large, unhewn black lava rocks. On the mosaic floor are inscribed the names of the largest concentration camps, and near the wall in the west burns a light.

In America

Many synagogues observe יוֹם הַשּׁוֹאָה with a special service. Usually six memorial candles are lit, one for each million Jews killed in the שׁוֹאָה. Sometimes survivors of the שׁוֹאָה are asked to light a נֵר זִכָּרוֹן. Other times, children of the survivors or other members of the congregation light a נֵר זִכָּרוֹן. In some synagogues, is a special six-branched menorah is lit on this day. After the candles are lit, memorial prayers are recited by the entire congregation. Often a שׁוֹאָה survivor addresses the congregation or there is a play depicting some of the terrible events of that period.

In Israel, יוֹם הַשּׁוֹאָה is a national day of mourning. An official ceremony takes place at יָד-וָשֵׁם, the memorial center for the שׁוֹאָה in יְרוּשָׁלַיִם. Everyone in the country observes a moment of silence. Radio and TV stations do not broadcast their regular programs. Instead, they have programs about the שׁוֹאָה all through the day.

Jews all over the world remember. Non-Jews remember too. All people of good will pray there will never again be such a period of destruction and horror.

נֵר זִכָּרוֹן

יְרוּשָׁלַיִם

מַחֲנֵה רִכוּז

YOM HA-SHOAH IN THE SYNAGOGUE

There is no specific blessing as we light the נֵר זִכָּרוֹן. Some people recite the Kaddish in memory of a relative or some other person who was murdered in the death camps. In April 1957, the Israeli Knesset passed a resolution proclaiming that the 27th day of נִיסָן would be the official שׁוֹאָה Day.

Today, every congregation chooses prayers and materials that reflect the mood and tragedy of the period.

The special Kaddish includes the names of the concentration camps and the ghettos.

אֲנִי מַאֲמִין
I BELIEVE

Special services are held in the synagogue on יוֹם הַשּׁוֹאָה. One of the prayers recited is אֲנִי מַאֲמִין, which expresses faith in God and in a messianic Age of Peace no matter what happens.

אֲנִי מַאֲמִין בֶּאֱמוּנָה שְׁלֵמָה	I believe with complete faith
בְּבִיאַת הַמָּשִׁיחַ.	in the coming of a Messianic age of peace.
וְאַף עַל פִּי שֶׁיִּתְמַהְמֵהַּ,	And though it takes a long time to arrive,
עִם כָּל־זֶה אֲחַכֶּה לוֹ	I still believe.
בְּכָל־יוֹם שֶׁיָּבֹא.	I will wait patiently until it is here.

YOM HA-SHOAH IN THE SYNAGOGUE

אֵל מָלֵא רַחֲמִים MERCIFUL GOD

The אֵל מָלֵא רַחֲמִים is the prayer recited at Jewish funerals.
Traditionally, it is also recited at Yizkor on some holidays.
The following אֵל מָלֵא רַחֲמִים is a variation honoring the
memory of the six million Jews-men, women and children-
who were murdered during the שׁוֹאָה.

אֵל מָלֵא רַחֲמִים הַמְצֵא מְנוּחָה נְכוֹנָה	Merciful God, grant perfect peace
עַל כַּנְפֵי הַשְּׁכִינָה,	under Your sheltering wings,
בְּמַעֲלוֹת קְדוֹשִׁים וּטְהוֹרִים	among the holy and pure
כְּזוֹהַר הָרָקִיעַ מַזְהִירִים,	who shine as bright as the heavens,
אֶת נִשְׁמוֹתֵיהֶם	to the souls
שֶׁל אַלְפֵי יִשְׂרָאֵל שֵׁשׁ מֵאוֹת רְבָבוֹת	of the six million Jewish martyrs
שֶׁנֶּהֶרְגוּ וְשֶׁנִּשְׂרְפוּ	who were killed, slaughtered,
וְשֶׁנִּטְבְּחוּ	and cremated,
בְּגָלוּת אֵירוֹפָּה.	in the lands of Europe.

**In the death camps of
Auschwitz, Treblinka,
Dachau, Mauthausen,
Ponar, Babi Yar,
Maidanek, Birkenau**

בְּגַן עֵדֶן תְּהֵא מְנוּחָתָם.	May they rest in Paradise.
יִצְרוֹר בִּצְרוֹר הַחַיִּים	May the merciful One bind their souls in
בַּעַל הָרַחֲמִים אֶת נִשְׁמוֹתֵיהֶם.	the bond of life.
יְהֹוָה הוּא נַחֲלָתָם.	Adonai is their inheritance.
וְיִזְכּוֹר לָנוּ עֲקֵדָתָם.	He will remind us of their sacrifice.
אֶרֶץ אַל תְּכַסִּי דָמָם.	The earth will not cover up their blood.
וְאַל יְהִי מָקוֹם לְזַעֲקָתָם.	Their cries will not be silenced.
וְיָנוּחוּ עַל מִשְׁכְּבוֹתָם.	May they rest in peace.
וְנֹאמַר אָמֵן.	And let us say: Amen.

WHY YOM HA-ATZMA'UT?

But the wheel of history continues to spin, and recent tragic and happy events have created new holidays to commemorate and remember.

For Jews, Israel Is the Center of the World

In 70 C.E. the independence of ancient יִשְׂרָאֵל came to an end. The Roman conquerors savaged the Holy Temple in יְרוּשָׁלַיִם and exiled many thousands of Jews from their beloved homeland. Some Jewish communities remained in יִשְׂרָאֵל, but large groups of Jews were forced to make their homes in different parts of the world. We call this time period the exile, for Jews were ousted, or exiled, from their land. But through the centuries of exile, Jews in far-off lands kept up the dream of the return to יִשְׂרָאֵל.

The Work of the Pioneers

The Arabs claimed Palestine and attacked Jewish settlements; the British refused to let more than a pitifully small number of Jews into the country. The חֲלוּצִים never gave up the fight for Jewish independence in their

YOM HA-ATZMAUT

own land, and finally they succeeded. The term צִיּוֹנוּת comes from the name of a mountain in יְרוּשָׁלַיִם, originally the site of the Jebusite fortress captured by דָּוִד הַמֶּלֶךְ. He built his castle on Mount Zion and later Solomon built the Temple there. The Second Temple was also built on Mount צִיּוֹן. Later, צִיּוֹן became a symbol for יְרוּשָׁלַיִם and יִשְׂרָאֵל. As it is said: "for out of צִיּוֹן shall go forth the Torah, and the word of the Lord from יְרוּשָׁלַיִם." At the time of Abraham, Mount צִיּוֹן was known as Mount Moriah.

The movement of צִיּוֹנוּת, founded in the second half of the nineteenth century, sought the return of the Jewish people to the land of יִשְׂרָאֵל as their national homeland and the creation of a political Jewish community there.

HEBREW WORD BANK

1	יוֹם הָעַצְמָאוּת	Israel Independence Day
2	הַתִּקְוָה	The Hope (National anthem)
3	אִייָר	Second month of the Hebrew calendar
4	מְדִינַת־יִשְׂרָאֵל	State of Israel
5	צִיּוֹן	Zion
6	מָגֵן דָּוִד	Star of David
7	חֲלוּצִים	Pioneers
8	יִשְׂרָאֵל	Israel
9	יְרוּשָׁלַיִם	Jerusalem
10	צִיּוֹנוּת	Zionism
11	דָּוִד בֶּן גּוּרִיּוֹן	David Ben Gurion
12	דָּוִד הַמֶּלֶךְ	King David
13	דֶּגֶל, דְּגָלִים	Flag, flags
14	סֵמֶל יִשְׂרָאֵל	Emblem of Israel

After the battle, this Israeli paratrooper prays at the newly captured Western Wall.

WHY YOM HA-ATZMA'UT?

On July 24, 1922, the British Mandate over Palestine was approved by the League of Nations. One of its conditions was the establishment of a National Home for the Jews, as stated in the Balfour Declaration.

The Declaration of Statehood

On Friday May 14, 1948 the leaders of the Jewish community in Palestine gathered in the Municipal Art Museum of Tel Aviv.

At one minute after midnight, the Mandate would end, but the Declaration of Statehood was to be made in the afternoon in order not to violate the Sabbath.

As the clock struck four, דָּוִד בֶּן גּוּרְיוֹן called the meeting to order. The assembly rose and sang הַתִּקְוָה, the Jewish national anthem, the prophetic words that were about to be fulfilled.

It was only after six million people were murdered by the Nazis, however, that the 2,000–year–old dream became a reality. On November 29, 1947, the United Nations offered the pitiful remnant of European Jewry a plan under which Palestine would be partitioned into two states—one Jewish, one Arab.

The Arabs Reject the Idea

On May 14, 1948, when דָּוִד בֶּן גּוּרְיוֹן stood up in Tel Aviv and declared the birth of the מְדִינַת־יִשְׂרָאֵל, the Arabs furiously attacked.

When the War of Independence was over, the newborn Jewish state was victorious. With the war's end, Israelis turned to the enormous task of building a new country. But the Arab world refused to admit that יִשְׂרָאֵל, even existed.

Did You Know?

High in the Judean mountains in the heart of יִשְׂרָאֵל stands the ancient and modern capital of יְרוּשָׁלַיִם. When King David unified Israel in the tenth century B.C.E., he made יְרוּשָׁלַיִם the capital of his kingdom. King Solomon, David's son, built the glorious Temple there. In 70 C.E. the Romans destroyed יְרוּשָׁלַיִם and for 2000 years it was ruled by conquerors. In 1948, after 2000 years of exile, the modern city of יְרוּשָׁלַיִם once more became the capital of the rebuilt מְדִינַת־יִשְׂרָאֵל.

סֵמֶל יִשְׂרָאֵל

דָּוִד הַמֶּלֶךְ

דָּוִד בֶּן גּוּרְיוֹן

דֶּגֶל יִשְׂרָאֵל

יוֹם־הַזִּכָּרוֹן, the Day of Remembrance, is a day of great sorrow. On this day, the fourth of אִייָר, we remember all the soldiers who were killed defending מְדִינַת־יִשְׂרָאֵל. Israel's יוֹם הָעַצְמָאוּת commemoration begins at sunset with a siren blast. A parent whose child died in the defense of Israel presents a torch to the President of the country, who uses it to light a flame in memory of Israel's fallen martyrs. Special prayers are said in the synagogue on יוֹם־הַזִּכָּרוֹן. At mid-morning on the fourth of אִייָר, sirens are sounded throughout Israel. Everything comes to an absolute standstill. Teachers stop their classes, and children put down their pencils and close their books. Cars pull over to the side of the road. Everyone stands silently at attention for a moment, sadly thinking of the brave men and women who gave their lives for Israel. A special ceremony is held on Mount Herzl, where torches are lit, symbolizing the eternal memory of the heroes.

At seven in the evening, another siren goes off. This signals the end of יוֹם־הַזִּכָּרוֹן and the beginning of יוֹם הָעַצְמָאוּת. The two days are joined together in recognition of the fact that without the courage and self-sacrifice of the fallen soldiers, there could be no יוֹם הָעַצְמָאוּת. Israel would not have been able to preserve its independence.

HEBREW WORD BANK

1	יוֹם הָעַצְמָאוּת	Israel Independence Day
2	הַתִּקְוָה	"The Hope"
3	אִייָר	The month of Iyar
4	מְדִינַת־יִשְׂרָאֵל	State of Israel
5	צִיּוֹן	Zion
6	מָגֵן דָּוִד	Star of David
7	חֲלוּצִים	Pioneers
8	יוֹם־הַזִּכָּרוֹן	Day of Remembrance
9	דֶּגֶל, דְּגָלִים	Flag, flags

The emblem of Israel consists of a menorah and olive branches. It tells us much about the ideals and history of the Jewish people. The Temple menorah reminds us of the ancient glory of the city of Jerusalem and its sad destruction. The olive branches are symbols of peace. They tell the world that Israel wishes to live in peace with its neighbors.

Getting Ready

As sirens sound all over the country at 7:00 p.m. at the end of יוֹם־הַזִּכָּרוֹן the national blue-and-white דֶּגֶל, which has flown at half-mast for the last twenty-four hours in honor of the nation's sacred dead, is hoisted by the Knesset (Israeli Parliment) guards.

דֶּגֶל יִשְׂרָאֵל

Let Joy Reign

Now Jerusalem begins to rejoice. There is dancing in the streets, and the night is turned to brilliant day by fireworks.

One of the most glorious days in the long history of the Jews came on the fifth of אִייָר, which in the year 1948 came on May 14.

On this day, Israel made the formal declaration of its independence. Every year, Jews all over the world—and especially in Israel—celebrate with excitement and joy the creation of the modern מְדִינַת־יִשְׂרָאֵל.

מָגֵן דָּוִד

Yom Ha–Atzma'ut Prayers

In synagogues in Israel and all around the world, special prayers in honor of יוֹם הָעַצְמָאוּת are added to the daily service. The services end with the blowing of the shofar and the recitation of special prayers.

מְדִינַת־יִשְׂרָאֵל

Yom Ha–Atzma'ut in the Diaspora

The excitement of יוֹם הָעַצְמָאוּת has caught on with Jews the world over. Jews everywhere celebrate the great day on the fifth of אִייָר each year.

חֲלוּצִים

 ## Did You Know?

דֶּגֶל יִשְׂרָאֵל THE FLAG OF ISRAEL

The Torah describes the flags of the twelve tribes of Israel, but there is no mention of a flag for the nation of Israel. In 1889 David Wolffsohn designed the flag of Israel that is in use today. He used the blue and white stripes of the tallit and added a מָגֵן דָּוִד in the center. The six-pointed star is known in English as the Star of David. Some people believe that King David had a six-pointed star on his battle shield.

סֵמֶל יִשְׂרָאֵל

YOM HA-ATZMA'UT IN THE SYNAGOGUE

There are no official or specific home יוֹם הָעַצְמָאוּת ceremonies. However, the Jewish Agency in Israel has published a Haggadah for יוֹם הָעַצְמָאוּת which borrows ideas from the Passover seder and applies them to the occasion. This new Haggadah compares Israel's independence after 2,000 years of exile to Passover, when Jews emerged from slavery to freedom. The vision of the return to our homeland has now become a reality.

PRAYER FOR THE WELFARE OF ISRAEL

OUR PARENT IN HEAVEN
אָבִינוּ שֶׁבַּשָּׁמַיִם

אָבִינוּ שֶׁבַּשָּׁמַיִם,	Our parent in heaven,
צוּר יִשְׂרָאֵל וְגוֹאֲלוֹ,	Rock and Redeemer of Israel,
בָּרֵךְ אֶת מְדִינַת יִשְׂרָאֵל,	bless the State of Israel,
רֵאשִׁית צְמִיחַת גְּאֻלָּתֵנוּ.	the first blossom of our deliverance.
הָגֵן עָלֶיהָ בְּאֶבְרַת חַסְדֶּךָ.	Shield it beneath Your wings of righteousness.
וּפְרוֹס עָלֶיהָ סֻכַּת שְׁלוֹמֶךָ.	Spread Your canopy of peace over it.
וּשְׁלַח אוֹרְךָ וַאֲמִתְּךָ לְרָאשֶׁיהָ,	Send Your light and truth to its leaders,
שָׂרֶיהָ וְיוֹעֲצֶיהָ,	officers, and counselors,
וְתַקְּנֵם בְּעֵצָה טוֹבָה מִלְּפָנֶיךָ.	and direct them with Your good counsel.

The prayer ends with a request for peace:

וְנָתַתָּ שָׁלוֹם בָּאָרֶץ	Give peace in the land
וְשִׂמְחַת עוֹלָם	and eternal joy
לְיוֹשְׁבֶיהָ.	to its inhabitants.

הַתִּקְוָה
HATIKVAH

The anthem הַתִּקְוָה **meaning "The Hope" was composed 1878 by Naftali Imber.** הַתִּקְוָה **is about the undying hope of the Jewish people through the long years of exile.**

כָּל עוֹד בַּלֵּבָב פְּנִימָה	As long as a Jewish heart beats,
נֶפֶשׁ יְהוּדִי הוֹמִיָּה,	The soul of a Jew yearns,
וּלְפַאֲתֵי מִזְרָח קָדִימָה	And toward the East
עַיִן לְצִיּוֹן צוֹפִיָּה;	An eye looks to Zion.
עוֹד לֹא אָבְדָה תִּקְוָתֵנוּ.	Our hope is not lost.
הַתִּקְוָה שְׁנוֹת אַלְפַּיִם	Our two-thousand-year hope
לִהְיוֹת עַם חָפְשִׁי בְּאַרְצֵנוּ,	To be a free nation in our land,
אֶרֶץ צִיּוֹן וִירוּשָׁלָיִם.	In Zion and in Jerusalem.

 ## Did You Know?

When you sing הַתִּקְוָה you are doing much more than just singing a nice melody. You are making a promise. You are promising that you will never forget that undying Jewish hope for independence. You are promising that you will do all within your power to help the State of Israel prosper.
You can help. You can buy products made in Israel, and you can plant trees in Israel by contributing to the Jewish National Fund. You can support Israel Bond drives. You can study the Hebrew language, and you can spend time in Israel as campers, students, tourists, and perhaps someday as *olim*—new immigrants to the Jewish homeland.
You can also help by learning about Israel and the Israelis and by studying Jewish history. The more you understand the Jewish homeland, the more you will learn to love and value Israel, and the more you will be able to do to help the survival and the growth of Israel.

יְרוּשָׁלַיִם

The following hymn expresses the strong feelings Jews have always had for Jerusalem, the city in which the Bet Hamikdash once stood.

מֵעַל פִּסְגַּת הַר הַצּוֹפִים,	From the peak of Mount Scopus,
שָׁלוֹם לָךְ, יְרוּשָׁלַיִם.	Shalom to you, Jerusalem.
מֵאָה דוֹרוֹת חָלַמְתִּי עָלַיִךְ	I have dreamed about you for a hundred generations,
לִזְכּוֹת לִרְאוֹת בְּאוֹר פָּנַיִךְ.	to be privileged to see your light.
יְרוּשָׁלַיִם, יְרוּשָׁלַיִם!	Jerusalem, Jerusalem!
הָאִירִי פָּנַיִךְ לִבְנֵךְ!	May your light shine upon your child!
יְרוּשָׁלַיִם, יְרוּשָׁלַיִם!	Jerusalem, Jerusalem!
מֵחָרְבוֹתַיִךְ אֶבְנֵךְ!	I will rebuild your ruins!

It's a Mitzvah 526

כִּי־תִקְרַב אֶל־עִיר	When you approach a city
לְהִלָּחֵם עָלֶיהָ	to make war against it,
וְקָרָאתָ אֵלֶיהָ לְשָׁלוֹם.	you must first ask it to surrender peacefully.
וְהָיָה אִם־שָׁלוֹם תַּעַנְךָ	If they agree to surrender
וּפָתְחָה לָךְ,	and open its gates,
וְהָיָה כָּל־הָעָם הַנִּמְצָא־בָהּ	then all its inhabitants
יִהְיוּ לְךָ לָמַס וַעֲבָדוּךָ:	shall be your prisoners

(Devarim 20:10-11)

יוֹם הָעַצְמָאוּת falls on the fifth day of the month of אִייָר. This day celebrates the declaration of Israeli statehood on May 14, 1948. Israel wanted to live at peace with its Arab neighbors, but they refused and attacked the newly created state.

The Torah tells us that it is a mitzvah to make an offer of peace before going to war. Unfortunately, the Israeli offer of peace was not accepted. Sadly, more than 14,000 Israeli men, women, and children were killed in the Arab–Israeli wars. Even today, more Jews are being murdered by suicide bombers.

YOM HA-ATZMA'UT IN SONG

REBUILDING

יִבָּנֶה We shall rebuild
עַמֵּנוּ Our nation
בְּאַרְצֵנוּ. In our own land.

DAVID KING OF ISRAEL

דָּוִד David
מֶלֶךְ יִשְׂרָאֵל King of Israel
חַי וְקַיָּם. Is alive and well.

LET'S DANCE

הָבָה נֵצֵא בְּמָחוֹל, Come, let's dance,
הָבָה נֵצֵא בִּמְחוֹלוֹת, Come, let's dance,
יַלֵּל יַלְלִי. La, la, la.

FROM JERUSALEM

כִּי מִצִּיּוֹן From Zion
תֵּצֵא תוֹרָה The Torah will emerge
וּדְבַר ה׳ And the word of Adonai
מִירוּשָׁלָיִם. Will emerge from Jerusalem.

MAY OUR EYES BEHOLD

וְתֶחֱזֶינָה עֵינֵינוּ May our eyes behold
בְּשׁוּבְךָ לְצִיּוֹן בְּרַחֲמִים. Your triumphant return to Zion.
בָּרוּךְ אַתָּה יְיָ, Praised are You, Adonai,
הַמַּחֲזִיר שְׁכִינָתוֹ לְצִיּוֹן. Who brings glory to Zion.

FRIENDS

הִנֵּה מַה טּוֹב It is good
וּמַה נָּעִים And pleasant
שֶׁבֶת אַחִים גַּם יָחַד. For friends to be together.

WHY LAG B'OMER?

The Jews of ancient Israel were farmers. Their lives depended on their crops. The time between Passover and Shavuot became a time of seriousness and prayer for the Jews. The farmer prayed to God for a succcessful harvest and a year of plenty and gladness. On the day after Passover, the priests in the בֵּית־הַמִּקְדָּשׁ would make a sacrificial offering of a measure of grain, called an עוֹמֶר.

The priest would mix the עוֹמֶר of grain with oil and frankincense and "wave" it up and down and from side to side in the בֵּית־הַמִּקְדָּשׁ.

HEBREW WORD BANK

לַ"ג בָּעוֹמֶר 1	Thirty-third day of the Counting of the Omer
עוֹמֶר 2	Sheaf, measure
לָמֶד 3	Hebrew letter with value of 30
גִימֶל 4	Hebrew letter with value of 3
סְפִירָה 5	Counting
בַּר־כּוֹכְבָא 6	Leader of the Jewish revolt against Rome
רַבִּי שִׁמְעוֹן בַּר יוֹחַאי 7	Scholar and teacher
יוֹם הַמּוֹרֶה 8	Day of teacher
רַבִּי עֲקִיבָא 9	Great Jewish teacher and leader
יְרוּשָׁלַיִם 10	Jerusalem
סְפִירַת הָעוֹמֶר 11	Time of the counting of the Omer
בֵּית־הַמִּקְדָּשׁ 12	Holy Temple

This ceremony was interpreted as a prayer for God to protect the harvest from strong winds and harsh weather. The Jews would count out the days between the waving of the עוֹמֶר and Shavuot.

We call these seven weeks (or forty-nine days) the time of סְפִירַת הָעוֹמֶר, which means "The Counting of the Omer." Orthodox Jews in Israel and the world over consider these weeks a time of solemnity. People do not go to parties, and weddings are not held. Special daily prayers are said.

Today in Israel many Jews travel to Meron on foot and by car to visit the grave of Shimon Bar Yochai. It is a tradition to sit around bonfires all night, telling stories and singing songs about Shimon Bar Yochai, Rabbi Akiva, and the hero Shimon Bar Kochba.

The Origin of Lag B'omer

On לַ"ג בָּעוֹמֶר we remember the faith and courage of the Torah scholars who lived in the land of Israel under the harsh Roman conquerors. The cruel Romans meant to wipe out Judaism, so they decreed: "Any Jew caught studying Torah will be killed!" This the Jews would not tolerate. The aged רַבִּי עֲקִיבָא, the greatest teacher of his time and a worker for peace all his life, was the leading spirit in the rebellion which now broke out.

WHY LAG B'OMER?

The military leader בַּר־כּוֹכְבָא was a brave and loyal Jew who seemed like another Judah Maccabee to his people. He and his troops captured יְרוּשָׁלַיִם and built an altar on the Temple Mount.

בַּר־כּוֹכְבָא

The Miracle of Lag B'omer

The armies of Rome were very powerful, but בַּר־כּוֹכְבָא won a great victory on לַ"ג בָּעוֹמֶר. The students and scholars who were his soldiers rejoiced. Another story tells that a terrible disease broke out among the students of רַבִּי עֲקִיבָא. Many young men died. But on לַ"ג בָּעוֹמֶר the disease suddenly stopped. That is one of the reasons we celebrate לַ"ג בָּעוֹמֶר.

Hadrian sent a powerful army, led by his best general. For two years they fought against the troops of בַּר־כּוֹכְבָא and finally drove the rebels into the town of Betar. When Betar fell (135 B.C.E.), betrayed by spies, thousands of Jewish fighters, including בַּר־כּוֹכְבָא were killed. To רַבִּי עֲקִיבָא, the life of the Torah meant more even than his own life. When the Romans found out that the rabbi was still teaching Torah, they took him away and tortured him to death.

רַבִּי עֲקִיבָא

Rabbi Shimon bar Yochai

רַבִּי שִׁמְעוֹן בַּר יוֹחַאי died on לַ"ג בָּעוֹמֶר, but on this holiday we remember not his death so much as his courageous and scholarly life, his faith and his bravery. We have picnics, outdoor games, and bonfires, remembering the rabbi's students who journeyed through the countryside to the cave of their great teacher, to which he had escaped after the unsuccesfull revolt.

We remember the hardships of רַבִּי שִׁמְעוֹן בַּר יוֹחַאי and his son, who suffered for the sake of Torah. In Israel on this day, many people travel all the way up to the high Mount Meron, where they visit the tombs of רַבִּי שִׁמְעוֹן בַּר יוֹחַאי and his son Eliezer. Everywhere in the land, people sit up late outdoors, singing songs about the great rabbi and about his teacher, the wonderful רַבִּי עֲקִיבָא.

לַ"ג בָּעוֹמֶר

Yom Ha–Moreh

In our own time לַ"ג בָּעוֹמֶר has become a time to honor teachers. On this day Hebrew and religious schools all over the country celebrate Yom Ha–Moreh, the Day of the Teacher. Special assemblies and parties are held, and often awards are given to teachers who have served in the field of Jewish education for a number of years. It is a special day set aside to tell our teachers how important they are to us and how much we love them.

עוֹמֶר

? Did You Know?

רַבִּי עֲקִיבָא RABBI AKIVA

(50 C.E. to 135 C.E.) Rabbi and martyr

As a young man, Akiva tended the sheep of Kalba Savua, a wealthy Jerusalemite who had a beautiful daughter, Rachel. Akiva and Rachel fell in love and wanted to get married but Rachel's father stubbornly opposed the match. He refused to see the young couple or to give Rachel a dowry when she left home to marry Akiva. Kalba Savua felt that Akiva, an unlearned shepherd, was not good enough for his daughter.

Soon after they were married, Rachel and Akiva had a son. When the boy was old enough to go to school, Akiva attended first grade along with him! So great was Akiva's yearning to learn the Hebrew alphabet and the Torah that he sat down with the small children to study. Along with the little ones, Akiva learned Hebrew, Bible, Talmud, and the commentaries. He progressed extremely quickly and soon became the best student in the school. With his wife's encouragement and blessings, Akiva left home to study Torah at the great academy in Lydda. He was forty years old at the time.

In twelve years, Akiva had become a great scholar. He even opened his own yeshiva in B'nai Brak. Now Akiva was a famous, revered rabbi whom others sought for advice.

The Romans ruled over Israel at this time with harshness and cruelty toward the Jews. The Romans issued strict decrees against the teaching of the Torah. But Rabbi Akiva defied the Romans and continued to teach. Rabbi Akiva encouraged the rebellion by the great Jewish hero, Bar Kochva.

The Romans imprisoned him and condemned him to death by slow torture. Akiva, eighty-five years old, bore his torment with a serene dignity. He was reciting the Shema as his soul departed.

שְׁמַע יִשְׂרָאֵל,	Hear, O Israel,
יְיָ אֱלֹהֵינוּ,	the Eternal is our God,
יְיָ אֶחָד!	the Eternal is one.

סְפִירַת הָעֹמֶר   COUNTING THE OMER

Before reciting the עוֹמֶר prayer say:

בָּרוּךְ אַתָּה יְהוָֹה,	Blessed are you, Adonai our God,
אֱלֹהֵינוּ מֶלֶךְ הָעוֹלָם,	Ruler of the universe,
אֲשֶׁר קִדְּשָׁנוּ בְּמִצְוֹתָיו	who has sanctified us with his mitzvot
וְצִוָּנוּ עַל סְפִירַת הָעֹמֶר.	and commanded us to count the Omer.

THE FORMULA FOR THE COUNTING IS RECITED:

Today is ———— of the Omer.   הַיּוֹם, יוֹם ———— בָּעֹמֶר.

The blank space is filled in differently every day:

יוֹם אֶחָד,	One day.
שְׁנֵי יָמִים,	Two days.
הַיּוֹם, שִׁבְעָה יָמִים,	Seven days,
שֶׁהֵם שָׁבוּעַ אֶחָד בָּעֹמֶר.	which was the week of the Omer.

The counting finally ends on the day before Shavuot:

הַיּוֹם תִּשְׁעָה וְאַרְבָּעִים יוֹם,	Today is the forty-ninth day,
שֶׁהֵם שִׁבְעָה שָׁבוּעוֹת בָּעֹמֶר.	which is seven weeks of the Omer.

It's a Mitzvah 302

וּסְפַרְתֶּם לָכֶם	And you shall count
מִמָּחֳרַת הַשַּׁבָּת	from the day after the Shabbat
מִיּוֹם הֲבִיאֲכֶם אֶת־עֹמֶר	from the day you brought the Omer
הַתְּנוּפָה	after the offering
שֶׁבַע שַׁבָּתוֹת תְּמִימֹת תִּהְיֶינָה.	seven complete Shabbatot.

(Vayikra 23:15)

According to the Torah, we are to count the עוֹמֶר for forty-nine days, starting from Passover and ending on Shavuot. The forty-nine עוֹמֶר days are filled with sad events which occurred during the period of Roman rule and the Crusades in the Middle Ages. During this period, it is customary to refrain from celebrations such as weddings. However, on ל"ג בָּעֹמֶר, these sad rules are suspended. Schools and synagogues enjoy picnics, with athletic events, games, and singing, and dancing, and weddings are permitted on this day.

WHY SHAVUOT?

The holiday that follows hard on the heels of Lag B'Omer is שָׁבוּעוֹת.

The name שָׁבוּעוֹת means "weeks," and the holiday falls exactly seven weeks after the second day of Passover, on the sixth and seventh days of the month of Sivan. (Reform Jews observe only the first of the two days.)

שָׁבוּעוֹת is a triple holiday; a threefold celebration that commemorates the giving of the תּוֹרָה on הַר סִינַי, the harvesting of wheat in Israel, and the ripening of the first fruits in the Holy Land.

A Torah Festival

As a תּוֹרָה festival, שָׁבוּעוֹת is also known as זְמַן מַתַּן תּוֹרָתֵינוּ. This means "The Time of the Giving of Our Law."

It was on שָׁבוּעוֹת that God spoke to Moses atop הַר סִינַי and gave the Israelites the עֲשֶׂרֶת הַדִּבְּרוֹת.

In the third month after they left Egypt, the Children of Israel came to the wilderness of Sinai. There they camped in front of the mountain. While they waited, Moses went up to God, and the Eternal called to him from the mountain, saying:

HEBREW WORD BANK

שָׁבוּעוֹת	1	Festival of Weeks
חַג הַבִּכּוּרִים	2	Festival of First Fruits
חַג הַקָּצִיר	3	Harvest Festival
עֲשֶׂרֶת הַדִּבְּרוֹת	4	Ten Commandments
אַקְדָּמוּת	5	Special Shavuot prayer
מְגִלַּת־רוּת	6	Book of Ruth
בִּכּוּרִים	7	First fruits
עֹמֶר	8	Measure of wheat
הַר סִינַי	9	Mount Sinai
זְמַן מַתַּן תּוֹרָתֵינוּ	10	Time of the giving of our Tora
תּוֹרָה, תּוֹרוֹת	11	Torah, Torot

You shall say to the Children of Israel: "You saw what I did to the Egyptians, and how I saved you and brought you to Me. Now, if you will listen to My voice and obey My laws, you will be My treasure from among all peoples."

The Ten Commandments sealed a covenant between the young nation of Israel and the one God. No other nation had a code of laws so just and humane. The Israelites abandoned the ways of Egypt and dedicated themselves to live by this lofty code.

Moses told the people what God had said. And the people answered, "All that the Eternal has said, we will do."

The people sanctified themselves and waited for the עֲשֶׂרֶת הַדִּבְּרוֹת. There was thunder and lightning, and a thick cloud surrounded the mountain. Then the sound of a shofar blowing very loudly was heard and the people trembled. Then God spoke the עֲשֶׂרֶת הַדִּבְּרוֹת. The rabbis said that as God spoke, the words echoed around the world in many different languages so that the whole world could receive them.

הַר סִינַי

Harvest Holiday Too

Besides being a תוֹרָה festival, שָׁבוּעוֹת is a harvest holiday. In ancient times, the grain harvest was begun on the second day of Passover with the ripening of barley. On this day an עֹמֶר of grain was brought to the Temple as thanksgiving to God.

The forty-nine days from Pesach to שָׁבוּעוֹת were counted publicly, and this period is still called סְפִירַת הָעֹמֶר (counting the omer). A special prayer was, and still is, recited each day at the end of the evening service. This prayer counts the days in a distinctive way, referring to them as the first day of the עֹמֶר, the second day of the עֹמֶר, and so on, so that an accurate count of the days elapsed can be kept.

After seven weeks of counting came the harvesting of wheat–the last cereal grain to ripen. Thus שָׁבוּעוֹת is also known as חַג הַקָּצִיר, the Festival of the Harvest.

A successful harvest meant prosperity for the coming year–one more reason why שָׁבוּעוֹת was a happy festival in ancient Palestine.

עֲשֶׂרֶת הַדִּבְּרוֹת

חַג הַקָּצִיר

The First, Ripe Fruits

Just about the time the wheat was harvested, the first fruits began to ripen on trees and vine in Israel. The תוֹרָה commanded the farmers to bring their בִּכּוּרִים as an offering of thanks to God. In Jerusalem, at the Temple, our ancestors were grateful to God for a bountiful harvest.

The תוֹרָה says:

For the Lord your God brings you into a good land, a land of brooks of water, of fountains in valley and hills; a land of wheat and barley, and vines and fig trees and pomegranates; a land of olive trees and honey. (Devarim 8: 7–8)

Of these "seven kinds" every farmer was to bring his בִּכּוּרִים as a thank you offering to God. That is why one name for שָׁבוּעוֹת is חַג הַבִּכּוּרִים, the Festival of First Fruits.

חַג הַבִּכּוּרִים

LET'S CELEBRATE SHAVUOT

What do we do on שָׁבֻעוֹת ? We decorate our homes and synagogues with plants and flowers. The greenery reminds us that it is a harvest festival.

In the Synagogue

In the synagogue, in addition to the regular holiday service מְגִלַּת־רוּת is read on שָׁבֻעוֹת. The reason is that this beautiful story of faith and devotion took place during the harvest season. Moreover, דָּוִד הַמֶּלֶךְ was descended from Ruth.

The Book of Ruth

מְגִלַּת־רוּת is one of the Five Megillot. It is recited in the synagogue on Shavuot because its story is set in the harvest field and its leading character embraces Judaism. The story of Ruth took place in Judah around the twelfth century B.C.E. During a famine, a Judean man named Elimelech with his wife Naomi and their two sons Machlon and Chilion fled to Moab. Soon afterwards, Elimelech died and his two sons married Moabite girls.

Chilion married Orpah, and Machlon was wed to Ruth.

The sons also died, and Naomi, widowed and childless, decided to return to Judah. Her two daughters-in-law offered to accompany Naomi back to her homeland. Orpah, after much discussion, was persuaded to remain in Moab, but Ruth insisted on going with Naomi.

The Harvest Season

The two women arrived at Bethlehem during the spring grain harvest. The farmers were busy harvesting and cutting stalks of grain with sharp sickles. According to Jewish law, any grain that dropped was left for the poor, who were allowed to glean the stalks. Ruth joined the gleaners. Boaz, a wealthy farmer, saw Ruth gleaning in the hot sun.

At the *bikkurim* festival of the First Fruits, all the age groups of the kibbutz take part. The children wear laurel wreaths and carry baskets of fruits and vegetables, the young men and women dance in the fields, and the adults cut sheaves of grain and bring them to the platform. Around this central point, the entire kibbutz is gathered, and nearby there is a display of the produce of the soil—the fruit of the kibbutz harvest from its orchards, vegetable gardens, and planted fields.

HEBREW WORD BANK

1	שָׁבֻעוֹת	Feast of Weeks
2	עֲשֶׂרֶת הַדִּבְּרוֹת	Ten Commandments
3	אַקְדָּמוּת	Special Shavuot prayer
4	מְגִלַּת־רוּת	Book of Ruth
5	תּוֹרָה, תּוֹרוֹת	Torah, Torot
6	בִּכּוּרִים	First fruits
7	סְפִירַת הָעֹמֶר	Counting the Omer
8	דָּוִד הַמֶּלֶךְ	King David
9	עֹמֶר	Measure of grain

תּוֹרָה

He said to her, "All you have done for your mother-in-law is known to me. God will reward you for your kindness."

Boaz married Ruth, and she gave birth to a son named Obed, who was the father of Jesse, who fathered David, who became דָּוִד הַמֶּלֶךְ.

Akdamut

A special prayer chanted in synagogues on שָׁבֻעוֹת is called אַקְדָּמוּת.
It is a hymn thanking God for giving us the תּוֹרָה.

Shavuot Taste Treats

שָׁבֻעוֹת calls for eating blintzes (a kind of small rolled pancake stuffed with cheese), cheese cake, and other dairy delicacies. The custom of eating dairy foods symbolizes the fact that the תּוֹרָה is likened to "milk and honey."

And so, with שָׁבֻעוֹת, the happy holiday season comes to a close.
The wheel has come full circle, and we can echo the words of King Solomon, who wrote in Song of Songs:

דָּוִד הַמֶּלֶךְ

> For lo, the winter is past
> The rain is over and gone,
> The flowers appear on the earth
> The time of singing has come . . .

? It's a Mitzvah

עֹמֶר

וּסְפַרְתֶּם לָכֶם	And you shall count
מִמָּחֳרַת הַשַּׁבָּת,	from the day after Shabbat,
מִיּוֹם הֲבִיאֲכֶם אֶת־עֹמֶר הַתְּנוּפָה,	the day you bring the barley offering,
שֶׁבַע שַׁבָּתוֹת תְּמִימֹת תִּהְיֶינָה.	seven complete weeks.

(Vayikrah 23:15)

The holiday of שָׁבֻעוֹת is celebrated on the fiftieth day after Passover, on the conclusion of the forty–nine days of the סְפִירַת הָעֹמֶר.
Sefiroth, means "counting." Starting from the second day of Passover, a special counting of the Omer prayer is recited each day.
The Torah tells us to count the Omer for seven complete weeks, starting from the sixteenth day of the month of Nissan.
After leaving Egypt, the Israelites waited for forty–nine days to rid themselves of their slave mentality. On the fiftieth day, they were spiritually ready to receive the תּוֹרָה on the holiday of שָׁבֻעוֹת.

עֲשֶׂרֶת הַדִּבְּרוֹת

SHAVUOT AT HOME

הַדְלָקַת הַנֵּרוֹת שֶׁל שָׁבוּעוֹת
SHAVUOT CANDLE LIGHTING

On the first day of assembling the universe, Adonai created the light of wisdom. When we light the festival candles, we are saying, : Thank you for keeping us alive, and giving us the light and wisdom of the Torah"

בָּרוּךְ אַתָּה יְיָ,	Praised is Adonai
אֱלֹהֵינוּ מֶלֶךְ הָעוֹלָם,	our God, ruler of the universe,
אֲשֶׁר קִדְּשָׁנוּ בְּמִצְוֹתָיו,	who made us holy by the mitzvot
וְצִוָּנוּ לְהַדְלִיק נֵר שֶׁל יוֹם טוֹב.	by commanding us to light candles on the festival.
בָּרוּךְ אַתָּה יְיָ,	Praised is the Adonai
אֱלֹהֵינוּ מֶלֶךְ הָעוֹלָם,	our God, ruler of the universe,
שֶׁהֶחֱיָנוּ וְקִיְּמָנוּ	who kept us alive and well,
וְהִגִּיעָנוּ לַזְּמַן הַזֶּה.	and gave us the opportunity, to celebrate this occasion.

Its a Mitzvah 488

וְשָׂמַחְתָּ   And you shall rejoice
בְּחַגֶּךְ   on your festival.

Devarim 16:14

It is a mitzvah to rejoice on the three Pilgrimage Festivals: Passover, Shavuot, and Sukkot.
In the time of the Holy Temple, this mitzvah was fulfilled by making a pilgrimage to Jerusalem and bringing Bikkurim.
Nowadays, we rejoice by participating in temple services, meeting good friends, and getting together with family. Instead of Bikkurim, we find opportunities to help poor people and those with special needs.

SHAVUOT AT HOME

קִדּוּשׁ לְחַג הַשָּׁבוּעוֹת
KIDDUSH FOR SHAVUOT

The candle lighting is followed by the recitation of the special Shavuot Kiddush, which highlights the giving of the Torah
The special festival wording is printed in red.

וַיְהִי־עֶרֶב, וַיְהִי־בֹקֶר, יוֹם הַשִּׁשִּׁי.	It was evening and morning on the sixth day.
וַיְכֻלּוּ הַשָּׁמַיִם וְהָאָרֶץ וְכָל־צְבָאָם.	The universe and planet earth and all that was within them had been completed.
וַיְכַל אֱלֹהִים בַּיּוֹם הַשְּׁבִיעִי, מְלַאכְתּוֹ אֲשֶׁר עָשָׂה,	Elohim finished all the work of creation by the seventh day.
וַיִּשְׁבֹּת בַּיּוֹם הַשְּׁבִיעִי,	And Elohim rested on the seventh day
מִכָּל מְלַאכְתּוֹ אֲשֶׁר עָשָׂה.	from doing all the work of creation.
וַיְבָרֶךְ אֱלֹהִים אֶת־יוֹם הַשְּׁבִיעִי,	And Elohim blessed the seventh day
וַיְקַדֵּשׁ אֹתוֹ,	and made it holy,
כִּי בוֹ שָׁבַת מִכָּל מְלַאכְתּוֹ,	because then Elohim rested from
אֲשֶׁר בָּרָא אֱלֹהִים לַעֲשׂוֹת.	all the work of creation.

If the holiday begins on a weekday, start here.

בָּרוּךְ אַתָּה יְיָ,	Praised is Adonai
אֱלֹהֵינוּ מֶלֶךְ הָעוֹלָם,	our God, ruler of the universe,
בּוֹרֵא פְּרִי הַגָּפֶן.	who created the fruit of the vine.
בָּרוּךְ אַתָּה יְיָ, אֱלֹהֵינוּ מֶלֶךְ הָעוֹלָם,	Praised is Adonai our God, ruler of the universe,
אֲשֶׁר בָּחַר בָּנוּ מִכָּל־עָם,	who chose us from among all people
וְרוֹמְמָנוּ מִכָּל־לָשׁוֹן,	and raised us from among all other
וְקִדְּשָׁנוּ בְּמִצְוֹתָיו.	and made us holy with commandments,

נַתֶּן־לָנוּ, יְיָ אֱלֹהֵינוּ, בְּאַהֲבָה	and in love, gave us
(שַׁבָּתוֹת לִמְנוּחָה),	(Shabbats of rest),
מוֹעֲדִים לְשִׂמְחָה,	festivals of joy,
חַגִּים וּזְמַנִּים לְשָׂשׂוֹן,	and special days of gladness.

אֶת־יוֹם חַג הַשָּׁבוּעוֹת הַזֶּה,	the holiday of Shavuot,
זְמַן מַתַּן תּוֹרָתֵנוּ,	the time of the giving of the Torah.

(בְּאַהֲבָה) מִקְרָא קֹדֶשׁ,	God gave us (in love) this holy event,
זֵכֶר לִיצִיאַת מִצְרָיִם.	so that we may remember our exodus from Egypt.

כִּי בָנוּ בָחַרְתָּ, וְאוֹתָנוּ קִדַּשְׁתָּ,	You have chosen us and made us holy
מִכָּל הָעַמִּים.	among all the nations

(וְשַׁבָּת) וּמוֹעֲדֵי קָדְשֶׁךָ, (בְּאַהֲבָה וּבְרָצוֹן)	And gave us Your holy days of joy (and
בְּשִׂמְחָה וּבְשָׂשׂוֹן הִנְחַלְתָּנוּ.	your Shabbat with love).

בָּרוּךְ אַתָּה יְיָ,	Praised is Adonai,
מְקַדֵּשׁ (הַשַּׁבָּת, וְ)	who makes holy (Shabbat),
יִשְׂרָאֵל וְהַזְּמַנִּים.	Israel, and all the seasons.

SHAVUOT IN THE SYNAGOGUE

עֲשֶׂרֶת הַדִּבְּרוֹת
THE TEN COMMANDMENTS

On שָׁבוּעוֹת the תּוֹרָה portion containing the עֲשֶׂרֶת הַדִּבְּרוֹת is read.
In some synagogues it is customary for the congregants to stand and to repeat the עֲשֶׂרֶת הַדִּבְּרוֹת with the Torah reader.
Read the עֲשֶׂרֶת הַדִּבְּרוֹת in English or in Hebrew.

א. אָנֹכִי ה׳ אֱלֹהֶיךָ.	I am Adonai your God.
ב. לֹא־יִהְיֶה לְךָ אֱלֹהִים אֲחֵרִים עַל־פָּנָי.	You shall have no other gods before Me.
ג. לֹא תִשָּׂא אֶת־שֵׁם ה׳ אֱלֹהֶיךָ לַשָּׁוְא.	You shall not take the name of God in vain.
ד. זָכוֹר אֶת־יוֹם הַשַּׁבָּת לְקַדְּשׁוֹ.	Remember Shabbat and keep it holy.
ה. כַּבֵּד אֶת־אָבִיךָ וְאֶת־אִמֶּךָ.	Honor your father and your mother.
ו. לֹא תִּרְצָח.	You shall not kill.
ז. לֹא תִּנְאָף.	You shall not be unfaithful to wife or husband.
ח. לֹא תִּגְנֹב.	You shall not steal.
ט. לֹא־תַעֲנֶה בְרֵעֲךָ עֵד שָׁקֶר.	You shall not bear false witness.
י. לֹא תַחְמֹד בֵּית רֵעֶךָ.	You shall not desire the house (property) of your friend.

 ## Did You Know?

Seven weeks after leaving Egypt, the Israelites camped at the foot of Mount Sinai. Then, the Bible tells us, Moses climbed to the top of the mountain and stayed there for forty days and forty nights. There God gave him the עֲשֶׂרֶת הַדִּבְּרוֹת.

God also informed Moses that "if they (Israel) will keep My Commandments, they will be a holy nation." Moses informed the Israelites, and without a moment's hesitation they answered, "All that God has spoken we will do." The עֲשֶׂרֶת הַדִּבְּרוֹת have been an important part of your Jewish tradition. For 3,000 years you and your ancestors have been obeying God's laws. Each generation has repeated the same words: "All that God has spoken we will do." Now it is your turn to become a link in the chain of Jewish tradition. It is time for you to repeat the ancient words כֹּל אֲשֶׁר־דִּבֶּר יְהוָֹה נַעֲשֶׂה.

WHY TISHAH B'AV?

תִּשְׁעָה בְּאָב is the saddest day of the Jewish year. The word תִּשְׁעָה, indicating the day of the month, means "nine," and אָב is the ninth month of the Jewish year. Many of the tragedies of Jewish history took place on this day.

The First Temple Is Destroyed

On the ninth of אָב in 586 B.C.E., Solomon's beautiful בֵּית־הַמִּקְדָּשׁ in יְרוּשָׁלַיִם was destroyed. Nebuchadnezzar, the king of Babylon, sent his army to conquer the kingdom of Judah. The victors destroyed Solomon's בֵּית־הַמִּקְדָּשׁ and set fire to the rest of the city. After 400 years, the House of David had come to a tragic end.

The Second Temple Is Destroyed

Six hundred years later, in 70 C.E., on the very same day, the second בֵּית־הַמִּקְדָּשׁ was destroyed.
In 63 B.C.E. Pompey's Roman legions overran Judea and after a three-month siege captured יְרוּשָׁלַיִם. Although Rome seemed all-powerful, the Jews never gave up the dream of independence. Finally in 66 C.E. the people of Judea rose up in revolt against Rome, and after much fierce fighting regained control of יְרוּשָׁלַיִם. The following year a well-equipped, powerful Roman army invaded Judea. In 70 C.E. the Roman general Titus began the siege of יְרוּשָׁלַיִם. On תִּשְׁעָה בְּאָב, the Romans stormed the בֵּית־הַמִּקְדָּשׁ and destroyed the city. More than a million Jews died in the war, and tens of thousands were marched into exile and slavery.

This miniature from a fourteenth century French Bible shows the blinded king Zedekiah being led into captivity. Zedekiah's desperate rebellion against Nebuchadnezzar led to the Babylonian invasion of Judah in 587 B.C.E.

Bar Kochba Is Defeated

About sixty years later, Hadrian became emperor of Rome. He decided to rebuild the בֵּית־הַמִּקְדָּשׁ as a place of worship for Rome's pagan gods. Determined to destroy Judaism, he outlawed the study of Torah and many other religious practices.

Hadrian's decrees triggered a new revolt. In 132 C.E., under the leadership of בַּר־כּוֹכְבָא and Rabbi Akiva, the people of Judea defeated the Roman garrison.

Hadrian sent Severus, his best general, to crush the revolt. One by one, the Jewish strongholds were destroyed. בַּר־כּוֹכְבָא and his soldiers made their last stand in the mountain fortress of Betar. On תִּשְׁעָה בְּאָב in 135 B.C.E., Betar was overrun and the defenders were massacred.

The Jews of Spain

When the Arabs conquered a part of Spain in 755 C.E., thousands of Jews emigrated from North Africa to Spain. The Arab rulers welcomed the Jews and used their talents for their own advantage.

The Marranos

Under Arab rule, Jews freely practiced their religion and built beautiful synagogues and schools of learning.

Things changed when the Christians reconquered Spain. The Inquisition was set up to force the Jews to convert to Christianity. Thousands of Jews converted, but many of them continued to practice Judaism in secret. Those who lived as Christians before the outside world but as Jews in private were called Marranos.

Under pressure from the Inquisition, King Ferdinand and Queen Isabella ordered the Jews of Spain to convert or leave the country. Hundreds of thousands chose to leave. The expulsion from Spain took place on תִּשְׁעָה בְּאָב in 1492. By sea and by land, scores of thousands of Jews sadly departed from their homeland.

Ten of thousands of escapees were drowned at sea and many were murdered by pirates who stole their belongings.

יְרוּשָׁלַיִם

תִּשְׁרֵי

בַּר־כּוֹכְבָא

נֵר־תָּמִיד

בֵּית־הַמִּקְדָּשׁ

LET'S OBSERVE TISHAH B'AV

Although Judaism is not a religion that emphasizes deprivation and self-punishment, there are several fast days on the Jewish calendar.

These have been set aside to recall tragic events in the history of the Jewish people.

תִּשְׁעָה בְּאָב falls on the ninth day of the summer month of אָב and has a tradition–filled background.

The Lamentations of Jeremiah

אֵיכָה, a sad book of the Bible, is read as part of the synagogue service on תִּשְׁעָה בְּאָב. It describes the sorrow of the prophet יִרְמְיָהוּ, who lived through the destruction of Jerusalem by the Babylonians.

As יִרְמְיָהוּ looked upon the ravaged city, he compared its sorrow and desolation to that of a woman mourning her husband's death:

How lonely sits the city that was full of people,
How like a widow she has become.
She that was great among the nations
Has become a vassal.

Not only are the words of אֵיכָה sad, but the trope, or chant, in which it is recited aloud has a sad and mournful sound. In some synagogues on תִּשְׁעָה בְּאָב, the worshippers sit on backless benches or on the floor as a sign of mourning.

Some Jews observe the תִּשְׁעָה days before תִּשְׁעָה בְּאָב as a mourning period. During this time they do not buy new clothes, have their hair cut, swim, eat meat, or make weddings.

נֵר זִכָּרוֹן

And Close with Hope
The Sabbath following תִּשְׁעָה בְּאָב is called שַׁבָּת נַחֲמוּ.
On it we read the fortieth chapter of יְשַׁעְיָהוּ, which contains a dream of hope and comfort: "Comfort ye, comfort ye, my people, Saith your God . . .."

Tishah B'Av in Israel
In Israel on תִּשְׁעָה בְּאָב, many people gather at the כּוֹתֶל־הַמַּעֲרָבִי in the Old City of Jerusalem. This wall is all that remains of the Second Temple, destroyed by the Romans so long ago. Here people pray and hope that Israel today will have the strength to withstand all the enemies that seek its ruin.

יְרוּשָׁלַיִם

It's a Mitzvah 603

יְשַׁעְיָהוּ

זָכוֹר **Remember**
אֵת אֲשֶׁר עָשָׂה לְךָ **what was done to you**
עֲמָלֵק. **by Amalek.**
(Devarim 25:17)

It is a mitzvah to remember the evil that Amalek committed against the Jews after their Exodus from Egypt. They ambushed and attacked the unarmed Israelites as they peacefully marched through the hot desert sands.

The forces of history have eliminated the nation of Amalek, but sadly there are no lack of anti-Semites to take their place. In modern times, the Communists in Russia killed millions of Jews and outlawed the practice of Judaism. The catastrophe of the Holocaust witnessed the murder of six million Jews. Some of your friends and their families may have been impacted by this horrible event. Your brothers and sisters in Israel are being murdered by Arab terrorists. Here, in America, more than 3,000 Americans, were also murdered by Arab terrorists on September 11, 2001.

On תִּשְׁעָה בְּאָב, we remember all of our fellow Jews who throughout history have been murdered by the Amalekites, and we renew our vigilance never to become victims of anti-Semitism.

כּוֹתֶל הַמַּעֲרָבִי

עַל־נַהֲרוֹת בָּבֶל

BY THE RIVERS OF BABYLON

On תִּשְׁעָה בְּאָב in 70 C.E. the Babylonians captured and destroyed the city of Jerusalem.

The victors marched their defeated captives to the city of Babylon. On the march, the soldiers made the captives sing the songs of Zion. From the depths of their grief the exiles sang this song.

Today on תִּשְׁעָה בְּאָב we can see the gleam of a united and rebuilt Jerusalem. We can hear the song of joy and triumph of the new born State of Israel.

עַל־נַהֲרוֹת בָּבֶל,	By the rivers of Babylon,
שָׁם יָשַׁבְנוּ גַּם־בָּכִינוּ,	there we sat and wept,
בְּזָכְרֵנוּ אֶת־צִיּוֹן.	when we remembered Zion.
עַל־עֲרָבִים בְּתוֹכָהּ,	There, on the willows,
תָּלִינוּ כִּנֹּרוֹתֵינוּ.	we hung our lyres.
כִּי שָׁם שְׁאֵלוּנוּ שׁוֹבֵינוּ דִּבְרֵי־שִׁיר,	For there our captors demanded words of song,
וְתוֹלָלֵינוּ שִׂמְחָה:	and our oppressors joy:
"שִׁירוּ לָנוּ מִשִּׁיר צִיּוֹן!"	"Sing us a song of Zion!"
אֵיךְ נָשִׁיר אֶת־שִׁיר־יְהֹוָה עַל אַדְמַת נֵכָר?	How could we sing a song of Adonai on foreign soil?
אִם־אֶשְׁכָּחֵךְ יְרוּשָׁלָם,	If I forget you, O Jerusalem,
תִּשְׁכַּח יְמִינִי.	may my right hand wither.
תִּדְבַּק לְשׁוֹנִי לְחִכִּי,	May my tongue stick to the roof of my mouth,
אִם־לֹא אֶזְכְּרֵכִי,	if I do not remember you,
אִם־לֹא אַעֲלֶה אֶת־יְרוּשָׁלַם	if I do not raise Jerusalem above
עַל רֹאשׁ שִׂמְחָתִי.	my highest joy.

אֵיכָה AICHA

The scroll of אֵיכָה is read on תִּשְׁעָה בְּאָב.

אֵיכָה is the third of the Five Megillot. Tradition has assigned the authorship of the scroll to the prophet יִרְמְיָהוּ, who personally witnessed the fiery destruction of Jerusalem by Nebuchadnezzar in 586 B.C.E.

אֵיכָה consists of five kinot, poems that mourn the destruction of the holy city. Four of the kinot are acrostics in which each verse begins with one of the 22 letters of the Hebrew alphabet from א to ת.

In the first kinah, the holy city of Jerusalem is described as a woman in mourning. Israel is in turmoil. The Israelite leaders and even God have abandoned Jerusalem. The people are fighting for survival, and even resorting to cannibalism. Now the days of punishment are drawing to an end, and soon Israel's enemies will be punished.

אֵיכָה יָשְׁבָה בָדָד
1:1 Lonely sits the city

הָעִיר רַבָּתִי עָם
That was once crowded with people.

הָיְתָה כְּאַלְמָנָה
She has become like a widow.

רַבָּתִי בַגּוֹיִם שָׂרָתִי בַּמְּדִינוֹת
Jerusalem was once a power among nations.

הָיְתָה לָמַס.
Now she is just a slave.

בָּכוֹ תִבְכֶּה בַּלַּיְלָה
1:2. Each night Jerusalem weeps.

וְדִמְעָתָה עַל לֶחֱיָה
Tears flood her cheeks.

אֵין־לָה מְנַחֵם מִכָּל אֹהֲבֶיהָ
Among her lovers there is no one to console her.

כָּל רֵעֶיהָ בָּגְדוּ בָה
All her friends have betrayed her,

הָיוּ לָה לְאֹיְבִים.
Her allies have become enemies.

יהוה לְעוֹלָם תֵּשֵׁב כִּסְאֲךָ לְדוֹר וָדוֹר:
5:19 Adonai, You will rule forever.

לָמָּה לָנֶצַח תִּשְׁכָּחֵנוּ תַּעַזְבֵנוּ
5:20 Why have You forgotten us

לְאֹרֶךְ יָמִים:
for so long?

הֲשִׁיבֵנוּ יהוה אֵלֶיךָ וְנָשׁוּבָה
5:21 Please! Restore us close to Yourself.

חַדֵּשׁ יָמֵינוּ כְּקֶדֶם:
Renew and give us a new start.

כִּי אִם־מָאֹס מְאַסְתָּנוּ
5:22 Do You really despise us so much

קָצַפְתָּ עָלֵינוּ עַד־מְאֹד:
that you have abandoned us?